Being Human in Africa

American University Studies

Series XI
Anthropology and Sociology
Vol. 65

PETER LANG
New York • Washington, D.C./Baltimore • San Francisco
Bern • Frankfurt am Main • Berlin • Vienna • Paris

Augustine C. Musopole

Being Human in Africa

Toward an African Christian Anthropology

PETER LANG
New York • Washington, D.C./Baltimore • San Francisco
Bern • Frankfurt am Main • Berlin • Vienna • Paris

B
821
. M866
1994

Library of Congress Cataloging-in-Publication Data

Musopole, Augustine C.
 Being human in Africa: toward an African Christian anthropology /
Augustine C. Musopole.
   p.   cm. — (American university studies. Series XI, Anthropology
and sociology; vol. 65)
  Includes bibliographical references and index.
  1. Humanism—Africa, Sub-Saharan—History. 2. Man (Christian
theology)—History—20th century. 3. Philosophical anthropology—
History—20th century. 4. Christianity—Africa, Sub-Saharan-
History—20th century. 5. Mbiti, John S. I. Title. II. Series: American
university studies. Series XI, Anthropology/sociology; vol. 65.
  B821.M866   1994   233'.096—dc20   93-14315
  ISBN 0-8204-2304-1   CIP
  ISSN 0740-0489

Die Deutsche Bibliothek-CIP-Einheitsaufnahme

Musopole, Augustine C.:
Being human in Africa: toward an African Christian anthropology /
Augustine C. Musopole. - New York; San Francisco; Bern; Baltimore;
Frankfurt am Main; Paris; Wien: Lang, 1994
  (American university studies: Ser. 11, Anthropology and sociology;
  Vol. 65)
  ISBN 0-8204-2304-1
NE: American university studies / 11

The paper in this book meets the guidelines for permanence and durability of
the Committee on Production Guidelines for Book Longevity of the
Council on Library Resources.

Printed in the United States of America.

To my loving wife Annie Nachisale
who has supported me all along,
and
my dear brother Willie Chila Musopole
who encouraged me to think for myself,
this book is dedicated.

Acknowledgement

This book owes its inspiration and development to many people and institutions. It is virtually impossible to mention each and every one of them. I would like to express my gratitude to the President of Colgate University, Dr. Neil Grabois, and the Academic Dean/Provost, Dr. Bruce Selleck for a generous grant towards its publication. My thanks also go to my friend and compatriot, the Rev. Dr. Harvey Sindima of the Department of Philosophy and Religion at Colgate who kept prodding me on to have this work published. I cannot forget my supervisor Dr. James Cone, Charles Briggs Distinguished Professor of systematic theology at Union Theological Seminary in New York City. He nurtured me academically. My friend and fellow doctoral student, now Rev. Dr. Gideon Khabela of Federal Seminary, South Africa, with whom I spent many precious hours discussing theology.

I greatly appreciate the permission granted to me by Heinemann Educational Books of Oxford, England, and also by Dr. John Mbiti to print from the following: *African Religions and Philosophy, New Testament Eschatology in an African background* and "The Encounter of the Christian Faith and African Religion." in *The Christian Century*, Aug.-Sept., 1980.

It is my hope that this book will be found useful in clarifying some issues in the theological dabate taking place in Africa today, and thus help to take that debate a step further especially in regard to Christian anthropology. Lastly, but not least, my thanks go to the staff of Peter Lang for their patience and able guidance in the preparation of the manuscript.

Table of Contents

CHAPTER ONE

INTRODUCTION

This book is about an encounter between an African view of humanity and the gospel of Jesus Christ understood as re-humanization. It is concerned with the self-definition and understanding of the African peoples and how that definition and understanding is critical to the efficaciousness of the gospel of Jesus Christ in Africa. It is also a book about Christian anthropology in African theology. The critical question for me has been, and still is, how does African Christianity define and understand African peoples in a way that is humanizing, and, how can that view influence the shaping a humane life for the African people in the totality of their existence?

I chose to explore this subject of African humanity for a number of reasons. Firstly, it was because of an earlier interest in the concept of humanness[1] (*umunthu*) as understood in my own country of Malawi as a philosophical bridge between western and traditional education. Secondly, an attempt to understand the colonial impact on African humanity against the traditional view of humanness. And thirdly, the relevance of the concept of humanness to the Christian gospel for the construction of a culturally relevant doctrine of the human person. This interest goes back to a little over a decade ago. While writing my thesis for the Master of Arts degree (University of Malawi), I was struck by the anthropocentricism of the Chewa traditional worldview. The Chewa are the largest language group in Malawi, occupying the central and southern parts of Malawi and also part of Zambia and

Mozambique. There are more than ten ethnic groups in Malawi and, broadly speaking, they all share a similar perception of the world with the Chewa. Since I sought a theology relevant to the culture of Malawi, I began to wonder how such a worldview could be related to the theocentric worldview that I had inherited from the West through Christianity and had come to embrace as a Christian in the Presbyterian Church. The apparent conflict of the two worldviews at this crucial point (who should occupy the center of my existence and world?) in the orientation of my life and theology started to haunt me. It will be necessary at this point to situate this concern in a larger context.

Beginnings of the Quest

In 1979, I was appointed principal of Robert Laws Secondary School. The Malawi educational system was established by missionaries and was then, and still is today, generally patterned after the British public school system. Malawi was a British protectorate for seventy-three years.[2] During this time nothing was done to bring an indigenous educational philosophy to bear on the practice of the new form of education. Even after independence, no serious effort was exalted to radically indigenize the educational philosophy. As I reflected upon the aim of traditional [Malawian] education, I realized again that traditional education was centered around the concept of humanness. Humanness is that essential character defined by our culture as the sum of what makes a person authentically human. I also realized that the western type of education, as received and practiced in Malawi at least, placed less emphasis on humanness in its curricular content and focussed on intellectual knowledge for its own sake. The wholistic character of the initiation ceremonies, which constitute a major part of the educational program in the African traditions and crucial to the humanization process, cannot be understood unless the idea of humanness is recognized as both the foundation and goal, not only of the rites of passage, but also of human growth and development.

It further occurred to me that without this traditional emphasis our very sense of political, economic and social development as a people and a nation would be greatly undermined through compromise and distortion. Already an inversion of values was taking place. Instead of seeing humanity and the promotion of humanness as the goal of development, human beings were instead viewed as tools of development. Human beings were a resource, a material power not different from, say, electricity or fossil fuel or machinery. People were conceived more and more as part of the means of production. The physical structures were thought to constitute real development, and the well-being of the people (especially the poor, weak and ignorant) was becoming a secondary concern. The poor living conditions of those who are victims of the tenantship system that has developed with tobacco estates is a case in point. A fundamental alienation was taking place, foreshadowing the loss of humanness in daily human interaction. The political repression through fear and intimidation, the suffering inflicted on those who fall victim to the detention act and judicial system, are a few examples of the lack of humanness in our values.

I was not the only one who was concerned about this lack of emphasis on essential humanness in our western-style education. The elders who had been schooled in the traditional wisdom also expressed their dissatisfaction with modern education. One could hear them again and again say regretfully, "Our children have indeed learned, but they lack humanness." The problem, I began to realize, was in our whole approach to education, an education that emphasized materialistic knowledge without an equal emphasis on humanness. Traditional education made humanness the foundational principle of all knowledge and all knowledge had to be in service of it. In modern schooling, students knew more about everything else except themselves. While schools were under the churches, character formation was deemed an important function of education, but with independence and the secularization of education, that emphasis has been dropped by default.

Theology and theological education in Malawi, and possibly all over Africa, have not escaped the distortions that have affected our educational praxis. They too have tended to place more emphasis on intellectual apprehension, following a western logical mode, thereby failing to address African existential reality in the way Africans are conditioned to understanding it. The theology and education that is given has come from a cultural area whose worldview is conceived more mechanistically than spiritually.[3]

In Africa, since the rise of nationalism, the word *humanity* or *humanism* has been one rallying point for protest movements against all kinds of oppression: domestic, political, economic, cultural, racial, and tribal. The idea of humanity has also formed the core of political ideologies of several countries, especially those that have espoused socialist philosophy. The socialist philosophy of Leopold Sedar Senghor of Senegal is based on the concept of Negritude and African personality, while Julius Nyerere of Tanzania has based his philosophy on the concept of *Ujamaa*,

a Swahili word that means familyhood.[4] The former president of
Zambia, Kenneth Kaunda, has called his brand of socialism,
"Scientific Humanism." Many political leaders have identified the
concept of humanity or humanism as one that expresses in a vital
and dynamic way the aspirations of African people. Nevertheless,
it is paradoxical that in some of these countries, more often than
not, people often get sacrificed for unnecessary military hardware
or prestigious projects that remain inoperable and under-utilized,
while people become political pawns between rival political,
ethnic, regional, and ideological groups. And as the saying goes,
when two elephants fight, it is the grass that gets hurt. Even the
ideology of humanism can take on a life of its own without regard
for the people it is supposed to work for if theoretical
considerations are divorced from their practical base. Humanness
is a practical philosophy.

Among African theologians, Mbiti, more than most, has
attempted to provide a philosophical and religious basis for an
African view of humanity. In so doing, Mbiti has made a
significant contribution to the development of African theology in
general and to the African understanding of humanity in particular.
In accordance with his method, in which he insists that African
theology cannot be African without seriously engaging African
insights and philosophy, Mbiti has sought to discover the
philosophical basis of African sense of Common Life (ontology)
as the first step in the theological discourse.

Even though African sense of Common Life is Mbiti's
point of departure for discussing African philosophy and religion,
the Christian doctrine of humanity per se has not received his
foremost attention. Two of his articles deal specifically with the

African view of humanity, as do sections in his major works. However, anyone who has read his works comprehensively will note that the reality of African humanity is at their center. His phenomenological approach makes this emphasis abundantly clearly. Mbiti is not an abstract theoretician but a historically engaged scholar who is interested in his subject for the existential realities he has encountered in his own life and observed in the lives of the African peoples. By discussing African humanity in the context of its cultural, philosophical, religious and historical manifestations, Mbiti clearly implies that Africa humanity cannot be understood without taking these realities into account. Furthermore, he intends that even Christian anthropology must emerge out of this same context. This latter point is crucial when we see that Mbiti's vision of African humanity goes beyond culture and history. Because he finds his ultimate identity in Christ, he is unwilling to define and confine African humanity to its culture and history. This humanity must be set in the context of something/someone Ultimate, and he finds the Ultimate in the God of Jesus Christ, whom he identifies with the God, (not gods) of African peoples. Mbiti has argued that, like all human cultures and histories, African cultures and history are also moving towards a fulfillment in God.

Mbiti writes neither as a sociologist nor a psychologist but as an African Christian theologian, one who seeks to understand the world, and African humanity in particular, from the viewpoint of his identity with Christ who is the embodiment of the new humanity. Therefore, he is not satisfied with merely philosophical and cultural description or interpretations; he considers these inadequate as long as they are not fulfilled in Christ. While the philosophical and cultural understanding is vital, he does not consider it to be normative and final for a Christian anthropology. Christ is the norm. As culture is preparatory to the Gospel, so the philosophical and cultural understanding of humanity is preparatory to the new humanity in Christ. Just as the Gospel fulfills African culture redemptively, so does Christ fulfill African peoples and their self-understanding redemptively through the impartation of the new humanity. Therefore, to define African humanity without taking into account the historical reality of Jesus the Christ is, theologically, not only to distort the human reality but to depreciate it as well. However, to take the reality of Jesus into account, and to ignore the cultural and historical context gives us a myopic view of our humanity.

To avoid these two extremes, Mbiti uses the concept of time as the hermeneutical means of moving from the African sense of Common Life (ontology) as the norm in African traditional thinking to Jesus as the new norm in view of the new humanity that he inaugurates. The Christological significance of this concept of time is that Jesus is God's eschatological sign by which the African concept of time is reversed and given a new direction and dimension. It is through this reversal of time that Mbiti finds the solution to the dilemmas of African identity, of time and history, of cosmic disharmony, and of the cultural challenge of the West, and a hopeful future for African peoples.

Mbiti speaks eloquently of the need for relevance in theology, if Christianity is truly to be rooted in African cultural soil. In considering humanity, Mbiti thinks that the concept of time is the key that unlocks the meaning that the African assigns to his or her sense of being in the world. Mbiti states that the notion of time is not meant to explain everything, and while we note this disclaimer, the primary question for this study is: Have we really stumbled on the key to our self-definition and understanding? If so, how adequate is this concept of time in unlocking greater part of our sense of being human in the world as African people?

Mbiti follows what I have called the dialogic-integrative method. His concern is for Gospel to enter into dialogue with African thought so that the two may be integrated into an African Christian thought system. As with other topics, Mbiti approaches the subject of African humanity phenomenologically. He first describes African humanity as it is expressed and expereinced in life and culture and then undertakes to interpret it by applying the concept of time. For Mbiti, time is not only key to the meaning of African sense of a Common Life (ontology), but also to understanding African philosophy and religion which are rooted in that sence of a Common Life.

Besides Mbiti and a few other male theologians,[5] the other major voices calling Africa's attention to the question of humanity are the African feminists.[6] The feminists are a small but growing group. Their agenda is bound to touch on many deep-rooted social and cultural prejudices and male-oriented cultural and social structures, thereby initiating a far-reaching cultural and theological revolution in Africa. How does Mbiti's interpretation of African humanity, in particular his concept of time, relate to this phenomenon? No relevant African theology can express its concerns for humanity while ignoring the concerns and humanity of women. The evil of sexism in our doctrines and church structures must be dealt with if the church is to develop a full and credible view of humanity. Mbiti makes a cursory mention of feminist concerns but has not addressed them fully anywhere.

Apart from being the subject of this book, African humanity has a very significant place in Mbiti's overall thinking. I will briefly highlight certain points here and leave the detailed discussion of each to be covered in its appropriate place in the book.

Mbiti takes very seriously the African worldview, which is exactly what most missionaries did not do. From it, he points out the centrality of human beings in the cosmic hierarchy. Humanity is in community with God and nature and with itself.[7] According to African thought, humanity is related to God through creation and thus human understanding and experience of God is bound up with human self-understanding as creatures. There is a Life as well as a knowledge of relationship between God and humanity. Therefore, the African view of God tends to be greatly anthropomorphic. However, Mbiti does not think this is bad because Africans are familiar with the spirit world and see a qualitative vitalistic difference between God and human beings.[8] They recognize God as spirit and humanity itself as priest of God on behalf of all nature. This is but one reason why Africans' experience of the world is a religious one. Such religiosity explains further the spiritual conception of the universe. In a sense, an anthropocentric view of what Harvey Sindima has called "Life-Together" (ontology) makes for a religion that is primarily for the good of humanity. Mbiti describes such religion as utilitarian. It has to do with humanness in relation to divinity on the one hand and to nature on the other. It is untilitarian because it is relational. Humanness authentically lived involves participation in the cosmic configuration of all living realities and relationships with a view to contributing to harmony, happiness, and the maintenance of moral integrity as the human vocation. This participation is fundamental to a human form of community where one finds one's place only in relation to others. Mbiti captures this religious outlook in his now-famous dictum: "I am because we are, and since we are, therefore I am."

While the dictum above defines African humanity in terms of itself, Mbiti does not think that it offers a sufficient understanding of an African sense of Common-Life. As I have said above, he rather finds the hermeneutical key in the concept of time which, I think is external though not entirely unrelated, to the African self-definition and understanding. However, for Mbiti the concept of time does not define African humanity ultimately. It is only Jesus the Christ who does.

Moral conduct is an important aspect in understanding humanity. Mbiti maintains that African people subscribe to the morality of conduct rather than to morality of being. The former is based on what one does, rather than on who one's essential being is. Africans certainly recognize an ontological or theoretical nature of humanity but they subject that nature to and see it through the concreteness of a lived situation in time and space. The disjunction between morality of conduct and of being is foreign to African way of thinking. This observation ties in with Mbiti's other idea that humanization is a process of realizing the human potential as defined by society. Mbiti thinks that the shaping of the individual socially, culturally, and morally is a continuation of the creation mandate to be human. One grows and blossoms into one's humanness or shrivels into non-humanness.

African people believe that human beings were created with

possibilities for immortality, resurrection, and rejuvenation, but
somehow all these possibilities were lost, rendering human beings
mortal. African peoples have sought to counteract this tragic
situation through corporate survival or corporate conquest of death.
In this connection, procreation is seen as a divine obligation and
children are regarded as the seed of immortality. Mbiti regards this
method as a failed attempt by human beings and African traditional
religion at realizing the lost paradise. Mbiti finds that this African
conception of humanity provides fertile ground for both Christian
anthropology and Christological formulation. He sees a mutual
relationship between biblical revelation and revelation in African
cultures. The former fulfills the latter while the latter is a
preparation for the former. Classical Christian theology defines
these as special and general revelations, and has considered that
each has implications for the other. However, when traditional
theology looked at extra-biblical religions, especially non-western
ones, often viewed these formulations of general revelation as
completely at odds with God's special revelation in Christ. Mbiti
reverses this trend, seeing the two forms of revelation as
continuous. In the light of this, the African view of humanity as
manifested in its socialization processes is complemented by the
biblical view with its high point in Jesus.

A succinct description that can unify Mbiti's thought on
African humanity is: *JESUS CHRIST, THE AUTHENTIC
MUNTHU IN AND ABOVE AFRICAN CULTURE IS THE
ULTIMATE IDENTITY FOR AFRICAN PEOPLES*. Mbiti writes as
an African cultural theologian. Because the cultural definition of
his Africanness is one of his great intellectual concerns, it is not
surprising that culture is one of his major theological sources,

dictating his method and constituting his major theological preoccupation. Mbiti sees the African people in their culture and the African culture in the people. To define the African, for Mbiti, is to describe him or her within the culture, but to define the African Christian is to place him or her in Christ and the African culture under Christ. By this method, Mbiti finds a way towards the realization of authentic humanity and community.

Mbiti's view of African humanity is dynamic; he takes into account the changes that have affected and continue to affect African humanity as a result of western Christianity, imperialism, colonialism, modernity and capitalism. He acknowledges that the sense of African identity is deeply confused (especially among urban elites) as a result of these forces. Does Mbiti's interpretation make it possible for people to hope for an authentic humanity? It remains to be seen.

Structure

This book is in six chapters. Chapter One deals with Mbiti and the dilemma of African identity. It explores his theological pilgrimage by attempting to identify formative factors, namely, his Africanness, his personal faith in Jesus, and his Anglican training, which have shaped his theological writings. It also surveys his major works and his theological method, which I have called, dialogic-integrative. I discuss his life and work under the rubric of the dilemma of self-identity. The main point of the chapter is that the embodiment of this dilemma is a major motivating factor in Mbiti's theological enterprise and leads to the centrality of the issue of humanity in his thought.

This dilemma of identity is not restricted to matters of

personal identity, but affects also the historical consciousness of the African people. Therefore, the second chapter focuses on the dilemma created by time and history for African humanity. It looks at the implications of the view of time that Mbiti has advanced and how he relates it to the person and work of Jesus. Prominent is the idea that time that moves backward reaches a dead end and can provide no hope for the present. It is only a Christ figure who embraces temporality in eternity who can reverse that trend. Because of this, Jesus is not only relevant to but needed by the African people as savior.

The dilemma of identity does not only translate into personal and historical terms, but into cosmic terms as well. In Chapter Three, I move on to discuss African myths of creation, the origins of death, the humanizing process, evil, and the spirit world. It is argued there that Mbiti is pointing to African attempts through traditional educational processes to work towards human integrity, which is a vital ingredient in the realization of personal, communal and cosmic harmony. It is concluded that Mbiti's dictum, "I am because we are, and since we are, therefore, I am," in its cosmic context makes an excellent summary of what it means to be human in Africa.

Chapter Four surveys the effects of change on African humanity since the European intrusion and through the colonial interlude. It is alleged in the chapter that this unwanted contact has not only precipitated the dilemma of identity but has also had a highly devastating effect on African humanity, resulting in devaluation of African personhood and worth. In the process fierce resistance has at times been triggered off to defend that humanity against further oppression and even extinction. African resistance to this European onslaught is examined, as is the challenge facing African governments to make good on the hopes of many people for a life of freedom with dignity. The proliferation of repressive regimes in Africa calls for a prophetic and political theology to assert the demands of the reign of God, sacredness of humanity, and the need for freedom and economic well-being as a prerequisite for the realization of authentic humanity.

In Chapter Five I undertake a critical evaluation of Mbiti's thought, leading to the conclusion that his concept of time has serious flaws and, therefore, proves inadequate as a hermeneutic key to African ontology. His assertions that Jesus is the bearer of authentic humanity is accepted, though for reasons slightly different from Mbiti's. It is proposed in this chapter that a better understanding of the cosmic context of African humanity is gained through the concept of Ontological Relationality. Jesus is not only foundational to an ontological relationality, but in him also the dictum, "I am because we are, and since, we are, therefore, I am," finds its authentic meaning and fulfillment.

Chapter Six attempts to provide some prospects for an African Christian anthropology using the idea of ontological relationality expressed through the concrete reality of humanness *(umunthu)*. The word, humanness, captures the African essence (especially among the Bantu speaking peoples) of human dignity and integrity, while negating all that dehumanizes. The chapter advocates a pragmatic and programmatic approach to the formulation of the African doctrine of humanness.

The contribution I expect this book to make is a modest one. In general, it seeks to highlight the foundational significance of the idea of humanity for theology, education, politics, economic and cultural development. More particularly, it seeks to advance African theology in the direction of doctrinal construction, in this case, Christian anthropology. It is also hoped that in the processes of attempting to achieve the above goals, it will highlight the contribution of a major contemporary African theologian whose work, despite certain limitations, deserves serious study and reflection.

CHAPTER TWO

IN SEARCH OF AFRICANNESS:
Dilemma of African Identity

> The only identity that counts and has full meaning,
> is the identity with Christ and not with any given
> cultures. Cultural identities are temporary, serving
> to yield us as Christians to the fullness of our
> identity with Christ.[1]

To hear Mbiti talk about some aspect of African theology
in general and African humanity in particular is to be in the
presence of someone who embodies the issues that he is talking
about. Mbiti has kept the relation of Gospel and culture at the
forefront of his theological task. This relationship comes out of his
method, a method that is a direct result of his existential dilemma
as a human being who is black and Christian on the one hand and
as one who belongs to a culture that has been marginalized on the
other. This relation can be seen in three significant sets of
methodological questions which he raises. The first is: "To what
extent can we find a theological meaning in tribal religions, and
having found it, relate it to Christian theology and life?"[2] The
second question is: "How can Jesus be a firm point of reference
and hold together the hopes embedded in the traditional
religion...?"[3] The third one is: "What Christological points arouse
interest? How does the person of Jesus fit into the African
conceptualization of the world and what points of contact does
New Testament portrait of Jesus establish with the African
traditional concepts?"[4] The Christo-cultural nature of these
questions points to where Mbiti's theological concern lies—the

identity of African Christianity. But that concern is on the public level; on the private and more personal level, Mbiti is concerned with his own identity as an African and a Christian. The theological use of a Christo-cultural paradigm camouflages on the public level, one suspects, a dilemma of identity for African people in general. It is this double dilemma, personal and collective, related but yet distinct, which sets out the parameters in which Mbiti expounds his African view of humanity.

Theological Pilgrimage

From the first time he heard the story of Dr. Aggrey of Achimota, in the then Gold Coast (now Ghana), it kindled in Mbiti a burning desire and ambition for education.[5] Like Aggrey, who had distinguished himself by earning the highest academic qualifications available, Mbiti wanted also to earn a college degree. Little did he know what that education was already doing and would keep doing to his African humanity. At first, he thought of pursuing a medical career but changed his mind. When he entered Makerere University College in Uganda in 1950, he pursued a liberal arts degree with majors in English and Geography and minors in History and Sociology. He knew that a degree was the key to better and well-paid employment, especially in the colonial service.

One day in 1951, while home on vacation from college, something happened that changed the course of his career plans. He was studying late one night (he still reads late into the night) when he saw a very bright light engulfing the kitchen of his home (the kitchen was a separate building from the main house). It was as if the kitchen had caught fire, yet it was not burning. The light vanished as soon as he noticed it. He was bewildered and yet aware of a Presence and a call to the Christian ministry. He says that he heard a word from within himself calling him to the ministry of the Word. This experience can be said to mark the beginning of his theological pilgrimage.[6]

In 1953, Mbiti graduated from Makerere University College with a Bachelor of Arts degree given by the University of London (to which Makerere was affiliated). In 1954, he was admitted to Barrington College, Rhode Island, in the United States of America, to study theology. He earned an A.B and a Th.B. and was there introduced to Western theological education. Like most of us from Africa who have pursued theological education in the West, he discovered that what he learned did not deal with questions that the African context was posing, and more personally, the question of what it meant for one to be African. The matter was both theological and anthropological. Consequently, he realized that the claim of Western theology to universality was deficient in many ways because it left out the cultural experiences of many people in the world.

From 1960 to 1963, he pursued a Doctor of Philosophy degree in New Testament studies at Cambridge University. His doctoral thesis is entitled *Christian Eschatology in Relation to the Evangelization of Tribal Africa*.[7] Three elements enshrined in this title, namely, eschatology, evangel, and tribal Africa, set Mbiti's theological agenda. On a personal level, Mbiti could identify with all three, but theologically his identity with tribal Africa was problematic at the time because tribal Africa had no theological base as western traditional theology was then taught. African culture was not theologically usable in traditional western theology that had been imported into Africa. But to exclude any culture at all was to exclude the people of that culture in the theological discourse. Therefore, Mbiti felt excluded from Western theological discourse and he fought to make himself a place in the world of theology in which he could theologize without using cultures other than his own as the media of communication. He alludes to this exclusion in this passage:

> Later, my theological studies in America and England did not challenge this position, [the idea that the African religious and cultural background was demonic and anti-christian] since that was not a living issue for my professors and fellow students. But upon my return to work in Africa, and upon careful study of the religious background of our people, there emerged gradually the demand to examine this issue and to form my own judgment.[8]

It was with more than academic interest that Mbiti sought to bring African culture into the theological discourse. It was also an act of bringing oneself into the discourse.

In 1964, he returned to Makerere to teach. He taught courses in New Testament and African Traditional Religion. He explains, "Since I myself had never heard any lectures on African religion, I set out to research on the subject in order to teach the course adequately."[9] It was more than simply an interest in teaching adequately that spurred him to carry out his research. It was, one suspects, a struggle to establish academic grounds to deal with the double problem of cultural and personal identity.

It needs to be remembered that at this time, independence had just come to many African countries and the matter of cultural identity was taking pride of place in the academy and on national political platforms. Even more significant is the fact that Mbiti's research confirmed to him very concretely that God's revelation was not *only* confined to the biblical record, but was *also* indelibly embedded in the African religion and culture. This word *also* was, as he puts it, "an extremely liberating word in my theological thinking." It raised for him "critical questions about the Western distinction between general and special revelation, and the idea of salvation history."[10] It became imperative for Mbiti that the concept of revelation be expanded so that African religious history could be conceived as an element in salvation history in conjunction with biblical revelation. This means that the biblical view of humanity was not the only view; it had to enter into a dialogue with the view from African cultural traditions in order to establish itself on African cultural soil.

Furthermore, Mbiti came to the realization that the religious culture of the African peoples, contrary to Western opinion, was actually the well prepared soil for planting the Gospel and that without that preparation, the Gospel would not have fared well. He declares categorically:

> It is in this complex of religiosity that the preaching of the gospel makes sense; it is this preparedness that has undergirded the spreading of the gospel like wild fire among African societies which had hitherto followed and practiced traditional religion. ...No viable theology can grow in Africa without addressing itself to the interreligious phenomenon at work there.[11]

By taking such a serious view of African culture, Mbiti was also taking his humanity very seriously, in contradistinction to the attitudes of a majority of missionaries and other Westerners.

In 1974, during the murderous and savage rule of President Idi Amin, Mbiti left Makerere to become Director of the World Council of Churches' [WCC] Ecumenical Institute at Bossey, Switzerland. His six year stay at Bossey brought him face to face with the ecumenical movement and its concerns. He observes: "It [the WCC] sensitized my thinking in many areas, one of these being the quest for Christian unity. I have seen the quest more sharply. ...The council made me aware, perhaps even frightfully so, of the problems of the world."[12] Mbiti was not a complete stranger to the ecumenical movement and agenda. He had been involved in some discussion on church unity in East Africa and was personally concerned with the evil of denominationalism. As is usual for him, Mbiti does not mince words on what he feels strongly: "It is beyond question that the church divisions are sinful. Many of them are created and sustained by the self-interests of church leaders."[13]

Mbiti realized while still with the WCC what he calls the "geography of salvation."[14] In addition, his consciousness of the ecumenical nature of the Church, religious pluralism, and theological complexities was sharpened, widened, and deepened. He developed a firm belief that it was only from a Christological basis that Christian unity can be forged. When he refers to Christology, he means not some abstract ideas about a past historical figure, but Jesus the Christ as a present saving reality personally experienced. Mbiti announces a desire to feel, think, and follow after this Christ as a personal pilgrimage into the lived reality of Christ then and now. He intimates, "I want to make a pilgrimage into Christ. I want to walk with Jesus of Nazareth on the shores of Lake Galilee and the hillsides of Judea, through the gates of Jerusalem. I want to see his healing hand, to hear his word that exorcises the evil spirits."[15]

Christ is the second factor in Mbiti's understanding of humanity. That determination comes, of course, from Mbiti's own Christian commitment. However, this Christian identity is not simply a matter of "take it or leave it"; it has to do with what is ultimate about being human. It is a movement towards the likeness or image of Jesus Christ. This movement is the essence of discipleship and it is through this commitment to discipleship that Mbiti expects true ecumenical fellowship to be found. Jesus becomes the common denominator for all particular cultural identities, thereby transcending while fulfilling them in the process. In my opinion, Mbiti is absolutely right to see discipleship as the lived basis for unity and fellowship. Discipleship is the way the Word continues to be made incarnate. Perhaps the tragedy of the churches is that they have many members, but few, if any, disciples.

Formative Factors

Three influences stand out as the most prominent formative factors on Mbiti's theological perspective: his Africanness, his personal faith in Jesus, and his Anglican ethos.
Mbiti's Africanness is manifested in his dogged insistence that African culture is a fundamental element in the doing of African theology.   He is primarily interested in local theological creativity. He wants a theology that bears the mark, **MADE IN AFRICA BY AFRICANS**. He is not keen on adaptations and he

rejects the term *indigenization*, claiming that Christianity is, from a historical point of view, already indigenous and not foreign. This claim absolves Christianity of the accusation of being a foreign religion. Western Christianity might be foreign but the Christian faith per se is not. Concepts that have a foreign origin, like Negritude and Black theology, are unacceptable to Mbiti. In other words, Mbiti rejects being associated with foreign identities in any ultimate way. His personal faith in Jesus translates into a Christocentric personal and Christian identity. It is Christ who defines Mbiti ultimately so that even his Africanness becomes secondary to this identity. Christ is the ultimate Savior and therefore, primary.

Three elements reflect his Anglican theological training. The first is the centrality of the sacraments in the experience of the Gospel as the new humanity in Christ. Mbiti finds the sacraments to be "Christocentric in their institution and practice" and says that they "epitomize the whole gospel, from the incarnation to the parousia."[16] It is participation in Christ that makes participation in the sacraments ontologically meaningful; otherwise, without Christ, they are magical in character. It is not only Jesus' word of institution that makes the sacraments significant, but his whole life. It is an incarnational Christianity that Mbiti advocates in his view of the sacraments. The second element is that of including scripture, tradition, and the living situation of the church (or reason and experience) in his sources for doing theology. These are traditionally Anglican points of emphasis. This second element can be subsumed under the term authority. It is obvious from Mbiti's writings that scripture is considered the primary seat of authority, followed by the church's tradition and the contemporary living church, in that order.

The third element is the comprehensiveness of his method.[17] For Mbiti it is not uniformity that matters, but rather complementarity. There is enough room for all types of theologies. Kwame Bediako refers to this as the "principle of theological freedom."[18] Authority can be legitimate only where there is freedom that allows and aids other people to fulfil themselves. The implication for humanity is that community and communion, authority democratically exercised, and freedom to be for others are all fundamental to a community of faith. Since the Anglican ethos is part of Mbiti's Christian commitment, it follows that only two factors are primarily operative in his theology, his Africanness and his personal faith in Jesus. This double identity emerges in his theology as a dialogical relationship between culture and Gospel. In relating these two, Mbiti is breaking new ground in the doing of theology. The theological dilemma that forced him to break this new ground consisted in missionary Christianity's *a priori* rejection of the cultural dimension of the African reality. In doing so, this imported Christianity rejected Mbiti's Africanness as theologically unusable and for it substituted Western culture. This resulted in a partial transposition of the perception of African humanity from an African to a Western worldview. In the view of western theological conditioning of the African church, the African Christian carries within his/her own body a theological question: Who am I?

Major Works

In his major works, Mbiti seeks to answer the question, who am I? He lays down that which constitutes his Africanness, the very things the missionaries rejected or Western scholars made simply a specimen for anthropological research.

Mbiti's written works have been in literature, African traditional religion, and African Christian theology. His published literature goes back to 1953. He has published poetry and novels in English and Kikamba, his mother tongue. However, our interest is in his theological works, where he has proved to be the most prolific African writer to date. His published articles began to appear in 1959.[19] Nevertheless, the challenge to greater theological productivity came on his return to Makerere in 1964, where he was appointed to teach in the Department of Theology and Comparative Religion.[20]

By training, Mbiti is a New Testament scholar, but at Makerere, besides biblical studies, he also taught African traditional religion as an area within comparative religion. The subject itself was very new for academic study, and thus there were no textbooks on it. To meet the challenge one had to create one's own textbooks; this is exactly what Mbiti did. The widely used *African Religions and Philosophy*, published in 1969, answered that challenge. Its subject is the human phenomenon in Africa from the perspective of African philosophy. In the same year, Mbiti published *Poems of Nature and Faith*, a small book in which he applied his poetic skill to religious themes of human origins, experience of life, and the reality of death. Reflected in this poetry is a rather pessimistic view of life in the face of death as viewed from within the traditional African religious perspective. However, this view is contrasted with the hope that the resurrection of Jesus brings.[21] Overall, his poetry carries his main theological message, which is the fulfillment of the African traditional religion in Christianity and African life in Christ.

In 1970 came another important book, *Concepts of God in Africa*. It was a welcome addition to the growing genre of literature on African religion written by African scholars. Mbiti has maintained that the missionaries did not bring God to Africa, but rather the God who brought them was already present in Africa. *Concepts of God in Africa* attempts to show the names, nature, and attributes of the God who was known by the Africans before the missionaries introduced the concept of God as conceived in western Christianity. Africanness is not independent of deity, but is defined in the context of it. To deny the Africans their knowledge of deity was to deny them the ultimate roots of their own identity. Mbiti reclaimed those roots and identified them with the God of the Christian scriptures as one and the same.

Love and Marriage in Africa was published in 1973. This book was written for the general public, especially the youth, from an African perspective. He wrote it to fill a felt need among the African youth who were ill-equipped in this particular area. He points out that the educational system neglected this important area of life while it catered to less important subjects. He laments this lack of preparation:

> Young people spend many years in schools and universities, learning how to dissect frogs, what happened during the American War of Independence or how to sing imported hymns in churches. But they learn little or nothing about their own human development, marriage and family life. ...In African traditional societies it was and is general practice to prepare young people for marriage and family but in the modern situation,

this is either never done or only done poorly.[22]

Sex education was a significant aspect of basic training in African educational practice. It was related to one's sense of being human in terms of physical development and the fulfillment of one's mission in the world. To neglect this emphasis in modern education is not only to undermine an important element of young Africans' education but also their sense of being human.

In 1974, Mbiti added another book on a significant aspect of African traditional religion. *Prayers of African Religion* is a collection of African prayers to which Mbiti provides a very comprehensive introduction.[23] He underscores the importance of studying prayers by pointing to the insights they give into various aspects of religious and philosophical thought of the African people. Mbiti says that through prayer humanity paints a spiritual picture of itself while posing at a religious moment.[24] In this book we meet African humanity as "notoriously religious."[25] This book on prayers, with the *New Testament Eschatology* and *Concepts of God*, form a trilogy, to use Kwame Bediako's expression, on the pre-Christian religious heritage.[26]

In 1975, the *Introduction to African Religion* was published. Its content overlaps with that of *African Religions and Philosophy* but is presented more simply. It is primarily aimed at secondary or high-school students but can be used in the first year of college.

A period of ten years elapsed before the next book appeared. The lack of a major work during this period was not because Mbiti had gone into hibernation, but rather because on his move to Switzerland he changed jobs and subsequently, even changed working languages. However, he wrote a number of articles in journals and contributed chapters to or edited books.[27] In 1986, *The Bible and Theology in Africa* was published. In this book the second stage of his methodology begins to appear, that is, the engagement of biblical revelation and African thought. It is an attempt to reconcile the two identities, African and Christian, that the one person embodies, and the two perceptions, African culture and Gospel, that the one faith must embrace. The synthesis he presents here is primarily between the African religious cultural identity and the biblical revelation. It is out of this engagement that Mbiti believes that African theology and, therefore, an authentic understanding of African humanity, are going to emerge. *The Bible and Theology in Africa*, is a methodological follow-up on the trilogy. It utilizes the content in the trilogy and engages it with the biblical and Christian formulations of the same themes in order to achieve an integrated view which is both African and Christian. This is the reason I call Mbiti's method "Dialogic-Integrative." The book is a methodological demonstration of how to relate African culture as *preparatio evangelica* to the biblical revelation in the hope of creating not only an African Christian theology but an African Christian identity as well.

Mbiti has to his credit about three hundred articles in journals and books. Some of his books and articles have been translated into French, German, Dutch, Korean, Spanish and Italian. He is currently working on a book that focuses on Christology. In it he intends to articulate more fully the phenomena of the encounter between the Christian faith and African religiosity. This encounter is his overriding theological concern.

Theological Method

In an article titled "Theological Impotence and the Universality of the Church,"[28]   Mbiti tells a story that is applicable to most, if not, all Africans who have gone overseas to study theology. In the story a young person returns to his village with a Doctor of Theology degree. There is an air of pride and great expectation among his people. They celebrate his return because his achievement is their achievement, too. Since he has mastered the secret of the whites, they expect him to help them deal effectively with the various threats to their well-being. Suddenly, as if fate also wants to test his accomplishment, his older sister becomes seriously ill. She is possessed. He suggests that they take her to a hospital, only to be reminded that it is fifty miles away. Something has to be done immediately, but he is very much at a loss. The chief says to him, "You have been studying theology overseas for ten years. Now help your sister. She is troubled by the spirit of her great aunt." He consults Bultmann, but does not find him of any help. Bultmann had demythologized spirit-possession in the New Testament. He is completely dumfounded and he cannot help even his own sister.

I think this story holds the clue to understanding the methodological principle upon which Mbiti has based his theological work. This principle arises, as the story indicates, from an existential dilemma felt by most of us trained in educational and theological institutions either established by western missions and/or abroad. What is this existential dilemma? Mbiti identifies it as the ignorance and impotence of western theology in the face of human questions in the churches of Africa.[29] Mbiti has turned the tables round by identifying the source of the problem for

African identity and theology and by putting the blame squarely on western theology, which has failed to engage African human questions. It is with the historical reality of the African people that Mbiti is concerned, not with abstract questions that western theology is so fond of posing.

Mbiti sees that part of the problem of the often-experienced existential dilemma is the negative attitude of the West toward African culture.[30] That attitude has limited the West's ability to perceive the cosmic and historical activity of God in Africa and among Africans. Mbiti explains, "The main negative result of using evangelism to put great stress upon cultural transformation, was that African converts were drawn away from their own cultural rooting. Hence their conversion took place largely outside of their cultural context;..."[31] The effect of this uprooting on the life of the church has been bad, Mbiti asserts, because church growth and development occurred also largely outside Africans' cultural grounding. Although the coming together of the Gospel and culture should have been the foundation of African Christianity, this phenomenon was aborted in the African context and with it also, African Christian identity. Western Christianity remains theologically, for all practical purposes, a foreign religion. Mbiti goes on to describe graphically what actually took place. He charges,

> Missionary culture told Africans in effect that "unless you are (culturally) circumcised, you cannot inherit the kingdom of God." So, unless they mutilated a large portion of their cultural foreskins, unless they became culturally westernized, and then Lutheranized, Methodistized, Anglicanized, Roman Catholocized, Presbyterianized,

> Africans could not inherit one centimeter of the christian
> faith. We were told that if we wanted Christianity (and this
> we had been persuaded passionately to want), we had to
> pay the price: we had to lay down our cultures, despise
> them as the missionaries did, condemn them as
> missionaries did, and run away from them since the
> missionaries had declared them to be dangerously
> demonic.[32]

This attitude is far from finished. Thousand of missionaries in
Africa are from theologically conservative churches that believe
that only their Western presence can keep the African Christian
faithful on the true path of faith without lapsing into syncretism.

Sources of Theology

Mbiti has identified six sources for the doing of theology
in Africa and they all contribute in some way toward the resolution
of the African self-identity dilemma. Mbiti identifies the following
sources as significant: The Bible, the theological tradition of the
church, the living experience of the church, the African religious
heritage, culture, and history.

1. *The Bible*

In a paper headed, "The Biblical Basis for Present Trends in
African Theology," which Mbiti delivered at the Pan-African
Conference of Third World Theologians, in Accra, Ghana, in
1977, he mentions that any viable theology must have a biblical
basis and that nothing can substitute for the Bible.[33] He agrees
whole- heartedly with the communique of the Pan African
Conference, which declares in part, "The Bible is the basic source
of African theology, because it is the primary witness of God's

revelation in Jesus Christ. No theology can retain its Christian identity apart from Scripture."[34] It is instructive here that Mbiti links the Bible to Jesus on the one hand and to the question of identity on the other. Jesus is the fulfiller, the one who supplies the missing end-piece of our identity as human beings. To this end the Bible is an important witness. Going beyond the communique, Mbiti sees the Bible as the word of God, which gives the kind of light needed in the search for meaningful Christian answers.[35] However, he warns that the Bible does not contain blueprint solutions to religious questions; hence, he sees the need for other, complementary sources.

2. *Theological Tradition*

In spite of the impotence of western theology to deal with the existential questions of African people and regardless of the fact that some of that theology proved oppressive and wrong-headed, Mbiti still believes that there is much to gain from the insights of that theological tradition. He writes:

> The older Churches, especially in Europe, have a rich inheritance of theological thought, scholarship, tradition, *instrumenta studiorum*, all of which we must utilize, since these are the resources that the Church through the ages has gathered and produced. It would be a sheer waste of time and energy if African theologians began to trace the paths of scholarship already so thoroughly trodden and explored by eminent thinkers of the older Churches.[36]

The reasons for seeking to maintain a base in the theological

traditions of Europe have to do with connecting to the mainstream
of ecumenical and apostolic heritage. By being thus connected,
Mbiti argues, the African theologians will not be isolated from the
catholicity of the church.[37] Even with this explicit endorsement
of western theology, Mbiti finds fault with African seminaries for
being content with western theology as it stands. He declares,
"Christian theology, too, must be understood in and translated into
the African milieu, if it is not to remain foreign and irrelevant to
the Church is Africa."[38] While accepting the need for
ecumenical, apostolic and catholic connectedness and identities, it
is not on the terms of the received tradition, but rather in terms of
where that tradition engages the African cultural context. The
Christian theological traditions are usable as a source as long as
they help in answering questions posed by the existential context
of the African people.

3. *The Study of African Religions and Philosophy*

African religions and philosophy form the context in which
theology in Africa can truly become African theology. The
primary question for Mbiti is: "To what extent is the Christian
message, as embodied in Christ Himself, seen as a fulfillment of
African religiosity?" The corollary to it is, "How far can we, or
should we, regard African religiosity as a *preparatio
evangelica?*"[39]

Mbiti anticipates a positive response to these questions.
Such a response would probably be the beginning of an
authentically African contribution, not only to theology at large but
also toward more appropriate structures by which the church can
effectively carry out its ministry. Confessional western theology

has uprooted African Christians from their cultural context, causing them to suffer from spiritual schizophrenia because it insisted that it alone had the truth and while all other religious persuasions were false. Mbiti rejects this assessment, retrieves African religiosity from the western theological garbage dump and makes it a vital source for African theology. Without this religiosity, theology in African would remain foreign and impotent.

African humanity cannot be divorced from its religiosity, and African Christianity cannot bypass it without ending up with a distorted African humanity, made not in the image of God but of Europe and America. Mbiti aims at an African identity that is made in the image of God, and for Africa.

4. *Theology of the Living Church*

Theological formulation is not a once for all time event, but is always provisional and ongoing, engaged with historical realities and responsive to changing circumstances. African humanity is not static either, but dynamic and growing. It has to distinguish itself through changing historical circumstances. The African church's search for selfhood can be said to reflect the human dilemma of identity and humanity's own search for authenticity. To talk about the living experience of the church is to talk about historical people and not an abstract collective. Mbiti warns that a church that stops reflecting constantly on the meaning of its faith soon dies of archaism and turns into a theological museum piece. Similarly, a people who refuse to take their destiny in their own hands risk being treated like an antique, a collectable for someone's aesthetic interests. Therefore, Mbiti takes the living presence of the church as another important source for doing theology. He observes, "This [the experience of the living Church] is what will test whether or not Theology is relevant to a given community and at a given time."[40]

The living experience of the church brings theology face to face with various historical situations and makes it historically accountable. Such situations may include poverty, famine, persecution, conflict and turmoil, development, religious pluralism, and many others. The church will endeavor to carry out her mission under these circumstances in faithfulness to her Lord and Savior. The theology emerging out of a particular situation will give the church a cutting edge, sense of direction, and relevance. Just as the church must live in the present, people too must live in serious engagement with the problems of the present. The dilemma of identity arises out of a tension between the past and the present, and it can be resolved by bringing the two dimensions of history and cultural expression under a higher and unifying perspective. For Mbiti, Jesus is that perspective.

5. *Culture*

Even though African traditional religion and philosophy arise out of and are aspects of African culture, Mbiti insists on distinguishing religion and culture for the very reason that the latter is the context of the former. Nevertheless, he does not separate them. African culture as context is a preparation for the Gospel. It is as context that it becomes one of the sources for the doing of African theology. As source, it gives to Christian theology its African particularity. On culture as context and source, Mbiti writes,

> Considering that Christianity is the outcome of
> culture and gospel, it is culture that shapes the
> different forms of Christianity. While in the
> southern two-thirds of Africa, the gospel was
> introduced in the cultural dress of Europe, it was
> inevitable that sooner or later there would be a
> cultural reaction from the African peoples. They
> now want to articulate the gospel, interpret it,
> celebrate it, and even suffer for it, within their own
> cultural framework.[41]

Mbiti commends the statement of the World Council of Churches
1973 Bangkok Assembly on the theme "Salvation Today," which
acknowledged that it is culture that shapes the human voice
answering the voice of Christ.[42] Therefore, culture has a dual
function in relation to African humanity. It is a theological
context for the Gospel and a source for theological reflection on
selfhood.[43]

6. *History*

To be human is to have a history. Besides needing cultural
rootedness, one also needs to be historically rooted. The whole of
African history is another source for theology in Africa. Mbiti
identifies three periods in this history. The first is the history of
the African people before the coming of the Europeans.
Archaeological finds are pushing that history back thousands of
years. The second period is that of European contact and eventual
effective occupation of Africa. The third phase is that of
independent nationhood. Theology is never done in a vacuum. It
has always the imprint of the historical times in which it is
produced. With the independence of African nations,

historiography in African has taken a new turn. The identity crisis for Africans has partly been due to a lack of historical rootedness. The history that the colonial education imposed on them was the history of the Europeans in Africa. Africans were told that they had no history apart from that of the Europeans. African history is no longer the history of the Europeans in Africa, but of the Africans. Of course, this includes our response to European presence. History as a source for theology has implications not only for the history of salvation but for African self-identity as well. Hence, more importantly for our purpose, historical consciousness is a significant factor in a people's self-definition. The historical questions are: How has God been active in the history of the African peoples and how has this history with God led to the definition of themselves as a people?

For Mbiti, African humanity is not only characterized by a dilemma of identity but also by multiple other dilemmas directly related to that of identity. He see African humanity caught up in dilemmas of time and history that raise the issue of historical consciousness, of cosmic and social harmony that has to do with human integrity and evil, and of modernity and change that aggravate the other dilemmas even further. Because of the nature of African perception of historical reality with its backward movement, he does not think it is possible to resolve the dilemmas. The reason for this inability lies in the fact that an important vital piece is missing from the African culture. The missing piece is supplied by Christianity. What this missing piece is, will be the subject of the next chapter.

CHAPTER THREE

A FUTURELESS HUMANITY:
Dilemma of Historical Consciousness

As previously noted, African Christians, according to Mbiti are marked by a double dilemma of identity: Africanness and Christian. This dilemma is not simply personal but is experienced also in the collective historical consciousness. While Mbiti thinks that his Africanness, in the form of African culture, and his Christianity should be allies, he acknowledges that certain factors have intervened to make them antagonists. Mbiti points to time as one of the intervening elements which has intensified acutely the African people's dilemma especially in the light of western linear conception of time. His interest in the concept of time is neither philosophical nor academic, but religious and theological. It has to do with the lived experience of people in relation to the spirit world. Only in this context can we appreciate why Mbiti gives time such a fundamental place in human life. However, more importantly for Mbiti as a Christian, it is in the context of Christian eschatology that the concepts of time and history have their ultimate theological meaning and value.

Source of Historical Dilemma

The way Christian eschatology has been presented to African people irritates Mbiti because it is partial, distorted, and robs African Christians of the full benefits of the Gospel. He points out that the Gospel was presented to Africans as a passport to heaven. The resulting view of eschatology is disruptive of the ordinary pattern of life and is of little relevance to the lived experience of African people. He remarks, "The presentation of eschatology directs the attention of Christians only to the next world, thus evading their responsibilities and involvement in Christian life here and now. ...This type of futuristic eschatology excels in and encourages hunting for signs of imminent end of the world."[1] Worse still, however, this futuristic orientation is not just a doctrinal matter to be assented to; it has become a mind-set of the African Christian community. Mbiti thinks that in part the distortion arose because the missionaries did not understand the African view of time and history, and in part from the way the biblical eschatological data has been translated and interpreted.

Time is very basic to the daily course of African life. Failure to take it into account is bound to produce serious dislocations in the psycho-spiritual, historical, and work orientation among African peoples. Consideration of the African concept of time is a methodological exercise necessary to discover what African culture can contribute in the development of an African Christian eschatology. The basic nature of the concept of time in African anthropology makes it significant for the encounter between the Gospel and African culture. The matter of time and history revolves around the questions: Where have Africans come from physically, theologically and culturally? And, Where are we going? Time and history have to do with the origins, present orientation and teleological end of humanity as these affect the meaning of human existence. In response to these questions, Mbiti demonstrates that human existence is determined by time that is conceived as going backwards, while Christian eschatology follows a linear view of time that is oriented towards the future. It is out of these two conceptions of the orientation of time that the African dilemma arises.

Mbiti brings three elements into play to highlight the role of the African concept of time in the experience of the African Christians for whom the dilemma is even more critical. The three factors are, the African (Akamba) concept, the missionary teaching, and the New Testament witness. He distinguishes missionary teaching from New Testament sources because the two are not the same in terms of authority and truth. He is not going to let the missionary or Western Christianity and theology be the final interpreters of the Gospel for Africans. Concerned with the need for an African theology, Mbiti advocates that Africans capture the sense of the Gospel for themselves. Therefore, his interest in the concept of time and history is not simply academic but is theological, motivated by pastoral concerns for the African community of faith.

From a pastoral theology point of view, the critical questions that lie behind the discussion of the concept of time relate to the compatibility between the African and Christian views and how the African view is an aspect of preparation for the Gospel in the Christian view. More concretely, the issue is how each view affects the daily life and actions of men and women. The incarnation makes the faith concrete. Mbiti intends to capture that concreteness for the African Christian by rooting Christian eschatology in the incarnation.

> A study of the New Testament shows that the heart of its eschatology is the incarnation which not only introduces the Christian differentia into Jewish eschatology (which forms much of the background), but makes it an intensely Christological phenomenon, so that eschatology has no meaning apart from Jesus the Christ.[2]

It is in the light of the difference that Jesus makes to time and eschatology that Mbiti deals with the dilemma in which the African view of time places its adherents. Let us look at some aspects of this historical dilemma.

1. *Human Ontology and Time*

John Mbiti approaches the interpretation of the African view of humanity from a philosophical and religious perspective. He finds the relationship between African traditional religion and African philosophy in religious ontology, that is, the spiritual interrelatedness of the universe. He makes the following observation, "Africans have their ontology, but it is a religious ontology, and to understand their religion we must penetrate that ontology. ...it is an extremely anthropocentric ontology in the sense that everything is seen in terms of its relation to man."[3] In this religious universe, human beings occupy a central place in their relationship to other beings. The critical question that Mbiti seems to be asking is: What is it that conditions the African people existentially? He finds the answer in the African peoples' understanding of time as what conditions them. It is in the light of this conditioning that Mbiti considers time to be the hermeneutical key to understanding the human reality in Africa. However, the hermeneutical character of time makes sense only in the context of spiritual relationships that exist in the universe. Mbiti goes on to assert that African peoples do not value time for its own sake, but because of what people do with it or how they relate to one another in it. The emphasis falls more on human utilization of time than on the essential nature of time itself. Therefore, for Mbiti, ...[The] concept of time may help to explain beliefs, attitudes, practices, and the general way of life of the African peoples, not only in traditional set up but also in modern situation (whether of political, economic, educational or Church life)."[4] Time becomes the organizing principle around which Mbiti interprets African human experiences. In this way, he gives us a glimpse of how the African people give meaning to their existence. Just as their actions define time, they similarly define themselves by their activity, which in turn make them agents of their own history.

We first come across the concept of time in Mbiti's writings in his doctoral dissertation [5]. One of his reasons for undertaking that study was to observe "the practical and theological consequences" of the encounter between Christianity and African traditional concepts.[6] In examining Christian eschatology against an African religious backdrop, Mbiti discovered that the African view of time not only had no comparable eschatology, but it had virtually no future dimension at all. Since time and history cannot be separated from eschatology, Mbiti further discovered that Christianity and African traditional religions exhibited fundamental difference in the conception of time and history. Christianity sees time and history moving forward toward a fulfilled end. African traditional religions see time and history moving backwards towards a literal and symbolic dead end. He also realized that the fundamental effect of the African view of time was to orient the life and outlooks of African peoples toward the past rather than the future. Since the missionaries did not bother to understand this view, they simply assumed that everyone perceived as they did and that their perception was the right one. It never dawned on them that there was a real conflict in perception which led to doctrinal misrepresentations by both sides. It is such an oversight by the missionaries and the resulting distortions in their presentation of the doctrine of eschatology to the African people that Mbiti is up against.

One such misrepresentation is the relationship of eschatology to future dimension of time. Because the African view of time lacks a future dimension, when the Africans come to Christianity, they must reverse time as they have previously perceived it, add a future dimension and make that dimension meaningful. It is in the meaning of the future dimension that Mbiti finds a basic conflict between missionary and African views. He sees missionary Christianity distorting eschatology, making it exclusively futuristic and severing the future manifestation of Jesus from his person and work, including the resurrection. In consequence of this separation, the Christian faith is transformed into a passport to heaven,[7] and the sacraments assume for the Africans magical significance, (charms to fortify one's life force).

The lack of a teleological end in the African conception of time, raises a dilemma for African people in view of their new awareness of a future dimension. The future dimension has a strong attraction because it can also be made materially meaningful.[8] It has become the dimension of material progress. In the Christian view, to have no teleological purpose is to have no meaningful end. Yet African religious perspective does affirm meaningful human living. That meaning is in this life, the present dimension of time, and not the future as presented by western Christianity. For the Africans, according to Mbiti, there is no human existence beyond the present period.

2. *Human Action and the Meaning of Time*

In defining the African concept of time as a "composition of events which have occurred, those which are taking place now and ... immediately to occur,"[9] Mbiti alludes to the anthropocentric nature of the African universe by tying the meaningfulness of time to human action instead of finding it in the independent existence of time. Mbiti claims that on its own, time does not move. It is human activity, and even more so, natural events that set time in motion. Human events have the special effect of bestowing meaning on time. In other words, time is humanized by them. By linking time with human activity. For instance, the milking of cows, taking them to the pasture, watering them, cultivating the gardens, harvesting, etc. Mbiti establishes a correlative relationship between them so that each affects the reality and operation of the other. By excluding from this definition events that do not occur through human agency but which depend on natural operations, Mbiti underscores further humanity's central role in assigning meaning to natural phenomenon. Mbiti makes this emphasis clearer when he says that time has to be experienced on the individual and collective levels in order to make sense. Since the future is not experienced, it cannot constitute time and therefore has no meaning. It is human action that makes time meaningful. In other words, history is the meaning of time and gives humanity a sense of rootedness in the cosmos. Since the future dimension of time has no historical form and therefore no cultural content, it lacks meaning. It is an illusion.

The two-dimensional African time, according to Mbiti, consists of a long past which he calls *Zamani*, and a relatively short, but dynamic present which he calls *Sasa*.[10] Implications for African humanity that can be drawn from this view of time are that its history and ontological expression are also two-dimensional, and that both are orientated toward the past. The meaning of human existence is governed by what is happening in the present and what has happened in the past. For Africans, the ideal in human history is to be found not in the future but in the past. It follows that African people can look only to the past for present inspiration. Being so dominated by the past, the ideal meaning of both life and historical rootedness is mediated through ritual repetition of the past.   Ritually, the wheel has to be constantly reinvented. Therefore, since African humanity has no time to look forward to, it can only face toward where it has come from. Mbiti states categorically that the Western linear view of time, with an indefinite past, a present and an infinite future, is "practically foreign to African thinking," and that people do not know what to do with such a time because they have little or no active interest in events that lie more than two years ahead.

Mbiti advances two arguments for maintaining that African thought and experience contain no future dimension of time. The first argument is based on linguistic evidence. An analysis of Kikamba, his mother tongue, does not yield for him a future dimension of time of any consequence. The second argument is based on the absence of myths in the whole of African having to do with a future dimension of time. There is, therefore, a radical disjunction in the conception of time between the Christian and the African views. One cannot even speak of the Christian view fulfilling the African view because the times in the two perspectives move in opposite directions. Something radical has to

be done to the African perspective in order to make it
compatibility with the Western linear view, before the African
view can be fulfilled.

We are told by Mbiti that African people look more to the
past than to the future for the orientation of their being. He goes
own to   assert that the African orientation of time, with its
movement from the present to the past, dominates every aspect of
life. The past becomes the center of gravity for human thought and
action. Without a future to look forward to and with a present
quickly disappearing into the past, the only sure time seems to be
the Zamani. Mbiti states:

> ...[T]he basic concept of time underlies and
> influences the life and attitudes of African peoples
> in the villages and to a great extent those who work
> and live in the cities as well. Among other things,
> the economic life of the people is deeply bound to
> their concept of time. ..[M]any of their religious
> concepts and practices are intimately connected with
> the fundamental concept of time.[11]

Even though people's activity defines time, the correlation between
time and human action means that people are caught up in the
seemingly cyclical rhythm of time; they go through the same
activities year in and year out. African humanity comes out not as
a master of time, but as a participant in time. "People expect the
years to come and go, in endless rhythm like that of day and night,
like the waning and waxing of the moon. They expect the events
of the rain season, planting, harvesting, dry season, rain season
again, planting again, and so on to continue for ever."[12] If the
world is not expected to end because there is no future dimension

in which that end can be realized, the continuation of time can only swell the Zamani period. It also means that the only meaningful time is the present, the period of intense living. It is in the present that all that humanity entails has to be realized before it is swept into the past, the graveyard of all history.

The Sasa period, which Mbiti calls the micro-time, has to do with the binding of individuals to their environment and thus is a period of conscious and intense living. Mbiti explains further, "Sasa is the most meaningful period for the individual, because he has a personal recollection of the events or phenomenon of this period, or he is about to experience them."[13] It is human consciousness that gives Sasa period its essential significance. Mbiti's interest in the Sasa fits his concern for practical theology. Only as it pays attention to the Sasa as the most meaningful period for the individual can the Christian faith be made accountable to the historical realities as they are experienced by African people. A futuristic eschatology removes that sense of accountability from the present to the future, from historical judgment to divine judgment. Instead of people taking their human responsibility of transforming their historical conditions seriously and in an engaged manner, they are resigned to their condition in the hope that God is going to change everything one day. Faith loses its relevance for the present where it is most needed. If faith is to be relevant to people, it is to be in this period, the time of intense and meaningful living.

The people who are in the Sasa also participate in the Zamani, while the Sasa slowly feeds the Zamani with the dead. Those in the Zamani belong to the macro-time; most of them are in the absolute past. They are in a time dimension that binds together all created things. With this period is linked the myths of creation, tribal origin, death, and myriad historical events that have gone into shaping the present way of life of all African people. Zamani is significant because it is the period that is populated with the spirits of the ancestors to whom the living are linked and owe so much. This linkage forms the strongest ontological pull towards the past.

The picture of the Zamani that Mbiti paints contains nothing that gives anyone hope for a better life. It is the dead end of human existence.

> So Zamani becomes the period beyond which nothing can go. Zamani is the graveyard of time, the period of termination, the dimension in which everything finds its halting point. It is the final storehouse for all phenomena and events, the ocean of time in which everything becomes absorbed into a reality that is neither after or before.[14]

Nevertheless, human ingenuity has invested the past with sacredness because Zamani enshrines the ancestors to and upon whom the living are related and dependent. People attempt through ritual to tap that sacred power for the present. This is one way of trying to overcome the reality of death, rejecting death's power to say the last word and affirming the triumph of life. In this way the past is imbued with a spiritual force that pulls the thought and actions of the African people to itself. But because the force is linked to the past, its power is only for conformity and not transformation. Since conformity assures one of security and order, Zamani gives security by providing the historical and ontological depth for the living. In this way African humanity is caught up in ritual time.

The humanizing process that begins in the Sasa period and has its final destination in the Zamani, illustrates the futility of a life without a teleological end. That process starts with birth, incorporation into society through naming, puberty and the attendant initiation ceremonies, marriage, procreation, old age, death, and incorporation into the community of the departed before attaining the status of ancestral spirit. The religious and ontological dimensions underlying this humanizing process are on one hand in the relationship between the living and the departed, that is, between those in the Sasa period and those in the Zamani period, and on the other hand, the relation of all these with God. The transition from the Sasa, the period of intense living, to the Zamani, the realm of the departed, Mbiti finds paradoxical. He wonders: "Paradoxically, death lies 'in front' of the individual, it is still a 'future' event, but when one dies, one enters the state of personal immortality which lies not in the future but in the Zamani."[15] Since the present can be extended to cover a person's entire life span, the paradox is apparent rather than real. It is in the period after death, in the state of personal immortality that Mbiti finds a real human dilemma for African humanity, as we will see later.

3. *African Humanity and History*

Mbiti's theological interest in history comes from his discovery that the God of the Bible was also the God whom the African people worshipped and, therefore, God's involvement with people was not restricted to Israel only. He argues persuasively,

> When we identify the God of Bible as the same God
> who is known through African religion (whatever
> its limitations), we must also take it that God has
> had a historical relationship with African peoples.
> God is not insensitive to the history of peoples other
> than Israel. Their history has a theological
> meaning.[16]

His interest also arises from his understanding of the nature of
African theology. Mbiti identifies two critical roles for African
theology. African theology has first to understand the African
people; then it can interpret to them the Christian faith. It is in the
context of theology's role of understanding that he places the
relevance of history:

> . . . [W]hile the Christian faith is the substance of
> the interpretative work of theology, and African
> Christians are the recipients as well as the agents of
> that interpretation, African theology has also to
> understand them. Thus African theology probes into
> African experience and reflection of life——the long
> historical heritage which has made us be what we
> are today, and the contemporary situation in which
> we are . . .[17]

For Mbiti, Salvation History is not a process independent of a
people's history. It is not imposed from outside their own history,
but is created within it and with it as they and God interact.

Mbiti has asserted that both the prehistory and history of
the African people are dominated by myth. This means that, "the
prehistory and history are telescoped into a very compact oral
tradition which is handed down from generation to generation."[18]
This telescoping generates myths that purport to speak about the

beginnings or origins of humanity, of the tribe, of the adventures and formation of a people. Mbiti reminds us that such an understanding of the past does not fit a mathematical time scale nor a scientific understanding of history. However, these myths provide a rationale for interpreting the universe and human life, and serve as paradigms for living. It follows that (pre-) history provides, according to Mbiti, the foundation for the current socio-politico-economic and religious relationships of the African people. People look to the Zamani because upon it the present rests.[19] It gives the people a sense of historical depth,[20] of ontological rootedness, of social solidarity, and of a relationship to the land.

Since time moves backwards, it follows that history too moves in that same direction. Mbiti states categorically: "In African thought, there is no concept of history moving 'forward' towards a future climax or towards an end of the world. ...The center of gravity for human thought and activities is the Zamani period, towards which the Sasa moves."[21] History moves backward, driven by the cyclic natural rhythm of time and human events. African peoples expect history to have no end because the natural rhythm of time seems to have no end and myths, associated with the Zamani, do not envision the end of the world. For African peoples, history continues indefinitely on its monotonous repetitious rounds as determined by the movement of natural phenomena and also of human events and activities. Like a roll of endless paper, time emerges out of the present and continues into the past as human events and activities leave their imprints on it, thereby transforming it into history.

On a more individual level, there is a concomitant natural time, which is transformed by personal life into personal history.

This personal history is characterized by cyclic rounds of "birth, puberty, initiation, marriage, procreation, old age, death, entry into the community of the departed and finally into the company of the Spirits."[22] The history of the community also follows an annual rhythm of activities determined by such natural events as rain, seasons, dryness, winds. Since the African peoples are mostly rural folk with agriculturally and pastorally based economies, the agricultural calendars are very crucial for their survival.

Time and history do not end at physical death, because existence continues beyond the grave. Mbiti states that when one dies, one enters the state of personal immortality which lies not in the future but in the Zamani.[23] First, one enters the category of the living-dead and finally one attains the status of spirit. This spirit existence is conceived to be almost the same as existence on this side of the grave, although somehow modified. It is closer to God and not subject to limitations of physical existence.

Mbiti asserts that death is a process that removes a person gradually from the Sasa to the Zamani.[24] The process begins from the onset of death. Yet, through remembrance by relatives the deceased[25] is kept alive historically and exits the historical stage only on the death of the last person who remembered that particular person. At this point, the individual ceases to be human and becomes a nameless spirit incorporated into a collective identity. This completes the process of dying and a state of collective immortality is achieved.[26] Mbiti describes this condition as:

> ...[T]he state of the spirits who are no longer formal members of the human families. People lose

personal contact with them... their names may still
be mentioned by human beings, especially in
genealogies, but they are *empty names* which are
more or less without personality or at best with only
a mythological personality built around fact and
fiction.[27]

Through incorporation into the spirit world a person exits out of
the historical state of being, where the past and the present
overlap, and enters the absolute past. Mbiti reiterates that such
spirits have no personal communication with human families. They
may, in some societies, speak through a medium, or become
guardians of the clan or nation and be mentioned or appealed to in
religious rites of local or national significance. In other societies
such spirits are incorporated into the group of intermediaries
between God and human beings. In reality, these spirits of the
departed, together with other spirits which may or may not have
ever been human beings, occupy the ontological state between God
and human beings. Human beings cannot go or develop beyond the
state of the spirits.   That state constitutes the historical and
ontological destiny of humanity in Africa. For Mbiti, however,
this is not a welcome end.

The living-dead is now spirit, which enters the state
of collective immortality. It has lost its personal
name, as far as human beings are concerned, and
with it goes also the human personality. It is now
an "it" and no longer a "he" or "she"; it is now
one of myriads of spirits who have lost their
humanness. . . Man is ontologically destined to lose
his humanness but gains his full spiritness. . .[28]

Mbiti regards this spirit state as subhuman rather than superhuman.[29] Even though such a spiritual state is above humanity in the ontological hierarchy, it is devoid of personality. Although it is near to God, it cannot attain to divinity. So the flow of historical consciousness back to the past does not ultimately lead to the lost golden age but to deterioration of one's humanity. "There is no teleology in African Eschatology; what there is might be called 'deteriology'——at least that is the theological and the philosophical conclusion to which our analysis seems to drive us."[30] African humanity becomes in the final analysis a hopeless tragedy of its own historical consciousness based on a sense of time that offers no future prospect or possibility. It is humanity caught between an unrepeatable past and no future at all.

African humanity suffers dire consequences arising out of the dilemmas of its conception of time and history. To assert that African view of time and history lacks a future dimension and that both time and history move backwards into the past is to deny Africans a sense of progress. Mbiti says that this is exactly the case: "... African peoples have no 'belief in progress,' the idea that the development of human activities and achievements move from a lower to a higher degree. The people neither plan for the distant future nor 'build castles in the air.'"[31] Further, just as the African historical sense lacks an idea of progress, so hope as a religious belief or doctrine does not exist among African societies.[32] Even though Mbiti does not deny that African people have hope, he does not think this hope has a transcendent and eschatological quality. Rather, it is temporal and short-lived, tied to utilitarian needs in a specific time or period as is worship. Therefore, African people have no hope for long-term events, and their sense of history lacks a teleological end.

The dilemma of time and history in which African humanity is wedged means that no new meaning can be created in history because the old mythical meaning remains dominant and one can only participate in the mythical meaning ritually. Being so dominated by the past African people cannot help but continue to think mythically and live ritualistically in order to be in harmony with the ancestral spirits. The African verdict on new ideas and creativity is that the "old wine is always better." They are conservatives.

African cosmology has situated human beings at a pivotal point in the configurations of the cosmos. It has fallen to human beings to give time a human character by actively participating in it. However, because they are caught in the movement of time instead of seeing themselves as above it and harnessing it to some sense of destiny, which is future and not the past, African people have become captive to time and are led to a dead past with a subhuman destiny. African people are collectively caught up in a backward roll of time and do not know how to reverse it. Unless something is done to the concept of time, Mbiti warns, people in Africa will remain backward-looking rather than forward-looking. They will remain without hope, unprogressive and prisoners of ritual and a mythical past instead of being makers of history.

Africans and Christian Eschatology

The picture of Christian eschatology that Mbiti paints stands in glaring contrast to the past oriented African "eschatology" of traditional religion. Even though eschatology is a new element in African Christian experience, Mbiti says that the

Africans have a feel for the Christian sense of eschatology. The lack of mythology about the future does not prevent African men and women from understanding the future-oriented myths of Christianity based on the historical concreteness of Jesus' life and resurrection. Mbiti finds the resurrection of Jesus to be the basis of Christian eschatology. He writes,

> This is the most decisive issue in the Christian faith, and without it the Faith, the Church, and the New Testament would be non-existent. ...It is the focal point for Christianity and the very kernel of the kergyma. Good Friday is flooded with meaning only in the light of Easter Sunday, and the event whose termini are the two days is a unity containing the one salvation phenomenon.[33]

In relation to the concept of time, the resurrection restores to the present what the past dimension of time has taken away and realizes what the future dimension of time promises. The effect of the resurrection on the African view of time is that, ...the future dimension of time is paralysed and neutralized by the resurrection; the past dimension of time is negated and reversed."[34] The feat of reversing time is possible because the resurrection is more than a temporal event. For Mbiti, it is a *presentization* of time dimensions, that is a bringing together in the present of both the past and the future.

Mbiti has delved into the nature of African time and history and how these have shaped African thought and action in order to combat false notions of eschatology that are influencing African Christianity. He is unhappy with both the African and Western paradigms of time in relation to eschatology because they all subject eschatology to time. For Mbiti, time is subject to eschatology in the New Testament: "Whenever Christians have reversed this order of priorities, they have ended up with a false eschatology as useless as the face of the clock without hands." While time is helpful in understanding the horizontal dimension of eschatology, Mbiti reiterates, eschatology has a vertical dimension that is non-temporal and therefore cannot be horizontalized. An adequate eschatological view of time must take into account the new fact of eternity in the human experience of time.

This eternal dimension in Christian eschatology is made possible by the incarnation of Jesus, in whom the spirit-world and human history touch. Because of the resurrection, Mbiti sees Jesus to have transcended all dimensions of time, and in the process to have made time one-dimensional.

> The prime N.T. emphasis on the nearness of the spirit world is on the encounter between the reign of God and the heart of Man. It is significant that the N.T. is silent on the spirits of the departed, apart from those who are in Christ. The incarnation brings the spirit world into the physical, so that the person who comes in Christ is enable to live simultaneously in both worlds.[35]

Mbiti tells us that this spiritual association with Jesus is different from mere surviving death by entering the Zamani. This Christian experience produces a living hope,[36] based not on nature's rhythms, but on God. Through the sacraments one has access into the spirit world; one does not have to wait for death to experience it. Through Jesus the human relationship to the cosmos is re-ordered—the cosmos is transformed from an anthropocentric to

Christocentric. God, who was regarded in the anthropocentric cosmos as "purveyor of moral power or Endless life" and always at human disposal, must in the Christian cosmos be loved for God's own sake. The individual is brought into close intimacy with God through the experiences of sacramental death, resurrection, and spiritual growth. The re-ordering of the cosmos means that God has to be first while human beings come second, and the world third.[37] In Jesus one is reclaimed from death and from subjection to passive survival, to become one of God's people.

Even though the African and Christian views of time are not compatible, in Jesus time has been reversed, so that both the past and the future are related to the present. That present is constituted by God's Eternal Now, by the God who is also the I AM.[38] Mbiti explains the experience of this eschatological time.

> The individual is intensely made to exist, for he is in the presence of God. This intensity of existence ignores or supercedes (I do not know which) the dimensions of time except the present. It means both the past and the future...are dissolved or assimilated in the present, for it is the presence of God and therefore completely irreducible.[39]

It is no longer human activity that gives meaning to time, but God who does. Mbiti's theology makes God in Jesus Christ the point from which all reality is viewed. He, therefore, finds both the African two-dimensional and the Western three-dimensional views of time inadequate to accommodate the Christian understanding of time, which has an eternal dimension. The anthropocentric worldview is also found wanting because it cannot account for a God who is cosmically active as its creator and upholder.

The inadequacy of the African view does not mean that it is theologically unusable. Mbiti insists that it has to be taken into account. By pointing out the inadequacy of the Western conception of time, Mbiti is warning that ideas from the West must be received critically. Both African and Western ideas must be subjected to the scrutiny of the biblical witness as exegeted with integrity. Jesus as the norm redemptively fulfills African culture and thought, that same culture that the missionaries thought was, for theological and practical purposes, outright demonic. Mbiti retrieves for theological use in Africa the spirit world, a force that pulls Africans to the past but which in Jesus is made a present reality.

Redeeming African Historical Consciousness

What are the practical implications of Mbiti's reconstruction of time and history for African humanity? It seems to me that Mbiti may be providing a theological route for solving the problem of the theological status of the ancestors in African Christianity. Since God has been involved historically with the African people, their history and culture take on theological significance. It is possible also to argue that following Mbiti's thinking, Jesus does not simply reverse time and historical orientation, but takes on the roles that were fulfilled by the ancestors. By reversing the flow of time and history, Jesus also liberates the spirits of the dead from 'deteriology' and puts them on the path to an eschatological goal of the reign of God in Christ. Since the eschatological experience begins when one encounters Jesus, people can continue to live intensely and meaningfully in the present for its own sake with the knowledge that the present time is the present of God's eternity, which eventually leads to a life that lasts. Mbiti intends that Christian people should be people of their time and history because God has made that time for them and is presently involved in it. An entirely futuristic eschatology denies this significance of the present, distorts the gospel, and robs people of their participation in the reign of God in the present. Abundant life begins in the present and not after death. This focus on life in the present leads us to the subject of the next chapter. In that chapter we will be able to see how the Africans have conceived of their life in the present in relation to their historical and spiritual roots in the past.

CHAPTER FOUR

QUEST FOR INTEGRITY AND COSMIC HARMONY:
Dilemma of Cultural Salvation

'I am, because we are; since we are, therefore I
am.' This is the summary of African human
relationships, on which is built the harmony,
happiness and morality of African societies.[1]

It was asserted in the first chapter that Mbiti embodies the
issues he is talking about and that his existential dilemma, created
by the collision of African and Western cultures, has given rise to
the search for a relevant theology that would suit his present
identity as African and Christian. In this chapter, I would like to
examine in some depth how he and all African peoples have come
to embody their Africanness. Mbiti is interested in African culture
not only as pure anthropology, but more because he is concerned
about the development of a relevant theology of the African
church. Crucial to his search for a relevant theology is the
discovery of theological meaning in tribal religions. For Mbiti,
theology has its source in the "spontaneous joy in being a
Christian, responding to life and ideas as one redeemed,"[2] He see
the first function of theology as understanding the people for
whom theology is done.[3] This means that Mbiti cannot do
theology without first understanding who he is as a person. As he
inquires into his identity as an African, he encounters his socio-
cultural, historical and religious world-view.

Mbiti also sees African humanity set firmly in the cosmic
configuration that encompasses other realities. Human beings are

at the center of this configuration; that placement points to their significant contribution in maintaining cosmic harmony. This cosmic harmony depends on the integrity of each being for its own sake and for the sake of all other realities. For human beings, integrity translates into moral justice in all dealings and relationships. Mbiti notes this connection between human beings and the physical world. "In African traditional world view the well-being of man is intimately connected with the well-being of the total creation. If a man abuses nature or the environment, nature also will abuse man."[4] Mbiti makes it abundantly clear that for humanity to be at the center in the cosmos does not mean that human beings are God or divine. Human beings are under the care of God as the overarching and surrounding reality. To be at the center also means being the meeting point, the crossroad in the relationship of all other realities. Thus to be human in African religious traditions is to carry tremendous responsibility towards the rest of creation. To underscores this point, Mbiti refers to myths of creation in which humanity is presented both as a creature made by God from clay and in some complementary myths as a creature from heaven with a home on earth.

Cultural Relevance

Since the primary theological task is to understand the people for whom theology is being done, it is logical that one should begin with historical human beings in the context of their culture. Mbiti avoids presenting an abstract description of humanity and opts for a flesh-and-blood presentation. This approach comes out of his conviction that God deals with people as they are culturally and historically, and not abstractly.

It needs to be said here that Mbiti's search for a theological human meaning in tribal religion has been prompted by Christianity's rejection of African culture. All African Christians have been formed by their cultures; indeed it is culture that makes them African. By rejecting African culture and teaching African / Christians to do the same, Western Christianity forced an impossible choice on them. As a result African Christians have lived with a contradictory double-consciousness, divided between two world-views, two traditions, and two ways of being human, that is, African and Christian, which had been presented to them as antagonistic to each other. The Western Christianity that rejected African culture superimposed on Africans the point of view of an alien culture while it denied the Africans their humanity which found expression in their cultural and historical consciousness.   African theology has the task of reversing this contradictory reality and reclaiming the African traditions in order to produce an incarnated Christianity that is relevantly African. One aspect of African culture that has been especially affected adversely by the imposition of norms from Western Christianity is the entire traditional humanization process which involves the inculturation of a people. Here, Western Christian doctrine was imposed without any regard for indigenous ways of thinking about what it means to be human. When salvation was interpreted as spiritual redemption more futuristic than present in its reality, African concern for the present for its own sake was underplayed; future expectations became more important than present historical realities. Salvation became individual and not communal. The new education systems were designed to de-culturate African Christians to meet the needs of Europe and

America, not those of the African Christians within their culture. Therefore, Mbiti attempts to underscore the significance of the African way of being human in the world because without it, African Christianity is superficial and African humanity is in subjection to a foreign theology and ideology.[5]

As a Christian, Mbiti's primary concern is to establish bridgeheads between the Gospel, as witnessed to in Scripture, and the African culture. It is only in this way that Christianity can be at home in African culture and vice versa. The closeness of the biblical world to the African world is an added advantage and all the more reason why African culture should have been taken seriously in the first place. However, Western Christianity intervened with its own culture through which the Gospel was mediated. Mbiti wants to remove this cultural mediation so that African culture and the Gospel can encounter each other. It is the aim of this chapter to show the possibility of that encounter in and through the traditional processes of one becoming human.

The Origins of Humanity

In the previous chapter, we saw that the historical consciousness of the African peoples begins with and is rooted in their myriad myths of creation. This historical consciousness manifests itself concretely as a religious way of being in the world among other realities with which one is connected in various ways. As Mbiti describes: "...African ontology is basically anthropocentric; man is the very center of existence, and African peoples see everything in its relation to this central position of man. God is the explanation of man's origin and sustenance; it is as if God exists for the sake of man."[6] This anthropocentric religious ontology is a relationship of God, Spirits, animals and plants, and phenomenal objects without biological life.[7] By asserting that in the nature of this unity the destruction of one ontological category would of necessity lead to the destruction of other beings including God, Mbiti describes the sense of harmony that is meant to exist in the cosmos and which the African community is supposed to reflect. It is incumbent upon humanity to maintain the social, moral and physical links with the rest of creation. Each ontological sphere is intended to maintain its own harmony as its share in the harmony of the whole cosmos.

For Mbiti, it is not only biblical myths which are theologically important, but all people's myths. In order to understand a people's beginnings and even their view of life, one has to deal with their myths. There are many myths of creation in Africa,[8] and according to these myths, human beings have one origin. They are created by God.[9] However, the myths of creation tell not only of origins but also tell how human beings relate to other aspects of the cosmos in their very being. Mbiti gives a few examples of these myths of creation. There are myths that tell of human beings being created from clay.[10] Such myths reveal as much about God as about humanity. God is the molder and human beings are creatures. Clay emphasizes human materiality and connectedness to the earth and everything found in it. The myths make a distinction between the nature of God and that of humanity. Humanity has a relationship both to God as spirit and to the earth as matter. To be human is to be both matter and spirit in living unity.

Another set of myths claims that human beings came from a hole in the ground. Myths that mention the hole conceive of the earth as a great womb. The underground is also often associated with the abode of the dead. The Tumbuka of Malawi refer to the graveyard as *Muzi-pasi*, meaning the Underground Village.[11] The earth is not simply dirt, but both the surface and the interior are spaces where the living and the dead have their abode respectively. Therefore, the land is highly charged with both creational and eschatological significance for African peoples. This explains why nd was the issue in many wars of resistance against white nation. To be human is to belong to the earth.

Other myths associate human beginnings with the marshes. The lic link here is with water and blood. Perhaps a connec made between the marshy water which is usually copper-co. from the oxidation of its iron content, and the blood that flows in human beings. Blood and water have much to do with life, human origins, and death literally and symbolically both in the Bible in and African traditions.

There are also myths that connect creation to a "Tree of Life." Trees are associated in many African cultures with sacred sites, medicinal plants, and theophanies. Shrines are usually constructed in a grove, and initiation rites take place in the bush. To be created from a tree is to be linked to the vegetative part of the world, which serves as a source of life and healing power.

One prevalent form of creation myths speaks of humanity coming down from heaven, either in a shower of rain or on a spider's thread. In this myth, human beings were made in heaven and were accompanied by God as they came into the world.[12] According to Mbiti, this myth places humankind in a position different from that of other earthly created things. Human beings come from "above," from another region of the universe, from a position "nearer" to God than that of other things.[13]

Mbiti cites other myths in which human beings are created as a pair, male and female, or husband and wife. In these myths, at the time of creation, God was very close to humanity. God was accessible and God enjoyed good friendship with all creation. Humanity was well provided for by God. Among the blessings that human beings enjoyed were foods of all kinds, shelter, protection, immortality, and even the ability to rejuvenate themselves. Mbiti likens this early existence to a state of paradise. God's providential care meant that other created things were placed at the disposal of human beings for the welfare of humanity. In these myths, we can observe that humanity is not an independent reality but rather a participant with other ontological realities in the life of the cosmos. Yet these myths emphasize that humanity, though related to other realities in the cosmos, is distinct from them, and that these realities exist for the sake of humanity.

Mbiti has looked at several of these myths of creation with a theological intent. He finds that the similarity of some of these myths to the biblical story is inescapable, supporting his contention that African culture is a preparation for the Gospel and those who thought it demonic and therefore unsuitable did so from cultural superiority and ignorance. Mbiti is interested to discover in African cultures and folklore theologically useful sources for developing African theology. In these sources one encounters a richness of imagery and conception about the origins of humankind in African thought, that Mbiti considers critical to any relevant theology and Christianity in Africa.

The myths of the human original state, says Mbiti, present a picture of harmony and tranquility. The state was paradisiacal in which immortality and resurrection were not only to be possible but normative as well. It was the "golden age. The theological significance of the myths is that human beings are created and sustained by the very presence of God, and that as creatures they are related in a fundamental way to the world. They are a sexual humanity so that they can perpetuate their kind through reproduction. Harmonious relationships characterized the state of human beings in the cosmos; by maintaining these relationships human beings would remain true to themselves.

The Coming of Death

Mbiti's major writings can be seen as an apologetic for African traditional religion in so far as he demonstrates close parallels between biblical and African thought while using traditional Christian categories. Such an apology was necessary because African religious thought and practices were under attack from Western Christianity and culture for the duration of the colonial period. The parallels between African and biblical thought are even more striking in the myths of how links between God and human beings are severed. Christian theology calls this severance the Fall of humankind and the act that led to it is Original Sin. This Fall in both African and biblical thought precipitated a quest for salvation. In African religious thought, the quest finds expression in the desire and search for restored harmony.

African mythology speaks of a fundamental cosmic dislocation, triggered by humanity, that adversely affected the cosmic configuration, especially the relationships between God and human beings on the one hand, and human beings and nature on the other. However, the dislocation's most tragic effects concerned human beings because death became a permanent reality in human experience. So, cosmic harmony was irreparably damaged. Even though various myths have different explanations for the cause of the break in relationship, they agree that a radical and tragic break took place.

According to the Kapirintiwa myth from the Chewa of Malawi, God withdrew from the community of human beings because of a bush fire. Human beings had discovered fire accidentally by rubbing two sticks together. The bush was set ablaze, forcing everyone to run for their lives. God withdrew to the sky and decreed that people would have to die in order to join God. Among the Ashanti of Ghana, it was a woman pounding *foufou* who kept knocking God with a pestle, thus causing God to withdraw to the sky in disgust. Some other myths make the breaking of a taboo the reason for God's departure from fellowship with humanity.[14] The myths differ as to what taboo was broken. Other myths point to the accidental removal by the hyena of the only means of reaching God. A basic theological point of these myths is that humanity's foolishness and lack of consideration for the presence of God, caused God's withdrawal into the sky.

The withdrawal of God from the community of human beings had dire consequences for humanity. The original state of existence was greatly disrupted. Enmity between human beings and animals became part of lived experience. According to the Kapirintiwa myth, the animal kingdom became divided between domestic and wild animals. The supply of food was no longer free, and the provision of immortality was lost. Disease and old age replaced the possibility of rejuvenation. The presence of death, brought about by the separation of God and human beings, was the most devastating ontological dislocation experienced by humanity. Death became an irreversible fact of life. Where life and its support system had been the norm, death and all forces of death now became normative. The earth became a place of death and only through it could humanity re-establish its links with God, not on earth, which had become the place of death, but in the sky. It was not only foolishness and a lack of consideration for God that brought about the separation, but also a disregard of God's word. This foolishness and disobedience were fostered by human selfishness which resulted in the destruction of the connection between the earth and the sky. The state of bliss that humanity enjoyed in the presence of God was shattered. This saying from the Fang people of the Cameroon is indicative of such a radical separation:"Nzame (God) is on high, man is below! Nzame is Nzame, man is man: Each to himself, each in his dwelling."[15] Of course, this saying also points to the ontological difference between divinity and humanity, but one cannot escape the impression of a radical separation in the relationship between God and human beings.

Mbiti claims that there are no African myths that offer a reversal of the tragic separation between God and humanity. African religions have failed to provide a future hope and the fulfillment of the African longing and cry for resurrection and immortality. He writes:

> Yet behind the glimpses of the original state and bliss of man, whether they are rich or shadowy, there lie a tantalizing and unattained gift of the resurrection, the loss of human immortality and the monster of death. Here the African religions and

> philosophy must admit a defeat: they have supplied
> no solution. This remains the most serious cul-de-
> sac in the otherwise rich thought and sensitive
> religious feeling of our peoples.[16]

Mbiti presents the failure of African religious practice to provide
a way to restore cosmic harmony as a dilemma of cosmic
proportions. Religiously, African people find themselves in an
existential dead-end. Human life is placed between life and death.
In order to be with God, human beings must ultimately face death.
So human beings must learn to live under the shadow of death.
The fact that African religions have failed at this critical point does
not mean that they are useless and must be replaced. Yet, this is
how Western Christianity considered them. The quest to regain the
lost harmony was seen as human attempts to achieve salvation by
human merit. The religion that produced such attempts was itself
considered an irreligious religion. Mbiti rejects this view of
African religions. He asserts that they are not useless but necessary
for the Gospel to perform its fulfilling function. For Mbiti, African
theology does not leave one the option of either/or but only that of
both/and.

It is in the light of this mythical background of separation
from the creator that Mbiti expounds the African view of a human
quest for cosmic harmony. This quest begins with the individual,
understood as a being-in-community, and extends simultaneously
to the whole community, society, the world and cosmos.
Communities invest their life and energy in the rites of passage
with a view to realizing a morally based society in order to ensure
harmony and happiness for the individual, the community and the
cosmos. The quest for harmony is manifested in communal rites

of passage, which take place at crucial points in a person's development. Humanization is the most appropriate term to describe this pursuit or process. The dictum, "I am because we are, and since we are therefore I am," is the cardinal philosophical principle underlying African communitarianism. This dictum is not simply a definition; it also refers to a process of being by becoming human. The process demonstrates how the dictum is understood at critical points in one's life.

Christianity has its own rites of passage, which as presented to Africans emphasize the spiritual dimension of life focused more on a futuristic salvation and less on the here and now.[17] The Christianization process that is presented as an alternative to the humanizing process in African traditions begins with baptism (infant or adult), receiving of the Holy Communion, marriage in church, establishing a Christian home, and dying in the faith. What Mbiti has struggled against is the simplistic designation of the African way as demonic and the Christian rites of passage as godly. (But many Western Christian rites of passage have European pagan origins.) African Christianity has as much to learn from the African culture as it has to contribute to it. The outlook of many African Christians has been shaped by the traditional humanizing process with its quest for harmony. African Christianity cannot ignore this cultural factor, but must come to grips with it.

Humanization

Humanization has to do with the inculcation and maintenance of human integrity or humanness. Integrity to their own humanity and to other cosmic realities is all human beings can contribute toward the realization of cosmic harmony. Even though death is the greatest obstacle to this harmony, human beings attempt to neutralize death ritually so that it does not have the last word. As a result, people are able to grope after life beyond the grave. Humanization is a process of being human by becoming human simultaneously marked by a number of crucial stages. Each stage in the humanization process has to do with the realization of more humanness. It is this process that shapes a people's minds and outlook. It is their educational, religious, political, economic and social training in becoming human. To understand a people is to enter into their humanization process so as to feel and identify with them.

Mbiti discusses the historical reality of human existence from the cradle to the grave and beyond by singling out the various stages during which initiation and/or the rites of passage take place. Becoming human is a process of physical and moral development; though no one completes it, each one is meant to strive toward its goal. In describing these rites of passage, Mbiti underscores the richness of tradition that African Christianity and theology must deal with. There is no point in dealing with European traditions when one cannot deal with one's own. Therefore, Mbiti, as an African Christian ans scholar, attempts to come to terms, at least phenomenologically, with African sociology, psychology, education, religion, politics and medicine. In this section, we will look briefly at the various rites of passage that Mbiti deals with in his works and see how they contribute to one's humanness and the achievement of communal and cosmic harmony. It is against the background of the cosmic community that one cultivates humanness.

1. *Kinship and Community*

The social nature of African humanity is maintained and expressed through extended family systems and elaborate kinship networks, which produce a very strong sense of community. Mbiti explains,

> The kinship system is like a vast network stretching laterally (horizontally) in every direction, to embrace everybody in any given local group. This means that each individual is a brother or sister, father or mother, grandmother or grandfather, or cousin or brother-in-law, sister-in-law, uncle or aunt or something else to everybody else. That means that everybody is related to everybody else, and there are many kinship terms to express this precise kind of relationship pertaining between individuals.[18]

This network of kinship relationships is greatly valued. To be human is to relate positively to others. It is to belong. In this context one's identity is understood only within the kinship network.

It is not enough to acknowledge the existence of kinship networks; the philosophy that underlies their functions must be appreciated. Since Westerners thought that only Western culture was capable of a philosophical mentality, they did not probe the African customs deeply enough to uncover their philosophical basis. Mbiti identifies the following functions as typical of any kinship network:

> a. It controls social relations as a means of knowing how people are related to one another.

b. It governs marital customs and regulations.

c. It determines behavior of one individual towards the other.

d. It is the basis of strong communal solidarity.

e. It extends to the animal, plant and metallurgical spheres through the totemic system,.

f. It extends on the vertical plane, to the world of spirits and finally to God.[19]

African kinship systems and their functions arise out of an African world view. In its theological task, the church ignores such a pervasive social structure at its own peril. The functions Mbiti identifies are in reality human beings in relationships. They are spiritual networks in which life and services flow towards each for the good of the whole. The kinship network has cosmic dimension and no individual can be properly understood without being placed in this context.

Genealogical information is also very important in the maintaining of kinship relationships. Genealogy helps establish relationships between individuals, households, families, and clans. To lack genealogical depth is to deprive oneself of one's historical rootedness, thereby diminishing one's ontological self-understanding. Furthermore, one's sense of being at home in the world is diminished. In relating the concept of time to genealogy, Mbiti points out that genealogies are a sacred means by which people orient themselves toward the Zamani; the recitation of genealogies links the living historically with the ancestors. In an effort to increase the sense of being at home and having social space in the world, African also practice adoptive kinship. One adopts people, especially personal friends, to whom one has no blood or marital relationship, as if they were kin and behaves toward them accordingly. Adoption is especially important in urban areas, where people have been uprooted from their rural kinship network. In this way people are able to recreate for themselves a sense of community to which they can turn for social sustenance and in time of need, just as they would in the kinship-network they have left behind. In rural areas, initiation rites help to create this adoptive bond within the particular class of initiates. Mbiti thinks that the nature of kinship networks could have been the bridgehead in introducing the doctrine of the Church as a community of faith, but alas, it too was ignored. Unless African theology can begin to deal with such networks, it risks creating a Christian community of individuals without a strong sense of belonging. This is one reason Mbiti insists that only Africans who have grown up in the culture are qualified to do African theology. It requires indigenous participation.

To a mind conditioned by the individualism so prevalent in West, the lack of individualism in African societies is a lamentable obstacle to initiative for self-development. Mbiti's response is:

> ...[T]he individual does not and cannot exist alone except corporately. He owes his existence to other people, including those of past generations and his contemporaries. He is simply part of the whole. The community must therefore make, create or reproduce the individual; for the individual depends on the corporate group. Physical birth is not enough: the child must be integrated into the entire society.[20]

In the process of incorporation into society, the community takes precedence over the individual, but individuality is still recognized. It does not mean that individual initiative and and identity are denied. The point is that only in terms of other people does the individual become conscious of his or her own being, duties, privileges, and responsibilities. Mbiti has captured well the sense of the individual-in-community in the dictum, "I am because we are, and since we are, therefore I am." As he says, this indeed is the cardinal point in understanding the African view of humanity. It is the ontological principle behind their sense of family, clan, tribe, nation and the cosmos. In light of the above, an African Christian cannot expect to have the same theological emphasis and outlook as a Western Christian whose view of life is individualistic and limited to personal history. Since the Gospel calls a community of faith into being, the African communal outlook forms a ready soil for such a community.

2. *Conception and Birth*

Physically a child enters the world as a morally neutral being. The baby may have the form of a human being, but humanness remains to be learned and realized. According to Mbiti, there is much more to humanity than simply the physical form. It is the society that helps one cultivate humanness. Preparations for the humanization process begin long before one's birth. Even though the event of birth belongs to the ever-recurring natural cycles, each birth is different because every child born is a unique being. Mbiti observes that "Nature brings the child into the world, but society creates the child into a social being, a corporate person. ...The birth of a child is, therefore, the concern not only of the parents but of many relatives including the living and the departed."[21]   Every precaution is taken during pregnancy to ensure the safety and strength of the child's life-force and protection against the forces of death because, as Mbiti says, "In the birth of a child, the whole community is born anew; it is renewed, it is revived and revitalized."[22]

In that unique life beginning to form and grow, the collective ontology of the whole community is involved. That small being is the promise of life through which the family, clan, and community is fulfilled and perpetuated. Bringing life into the world is a sacred act. Mbiti describes it as a divine obligation; children are the seed of that immortality lost to first human beings: "Children perpetuate mankind, they renew what is otherwise old and dying. They run ahead of death and shout: 'Life! Life! Life!'"[23]

Given the sacredness of bearing children, Mbiti finds it paradoxical that multiple births raise serious existential problems in some societies. He finds two attitudes toward multiple births among African societies. The positive attitude celebrates such births and treats them as a sign of fecundity and a source of blessing upon the community. Mbiti says that such children are thought to have special powers. In Central Africa, they are called "the children of God and heaven." The negative attitude regards such births as ominous because they are an exception to the rule. While it is accepted as normal for some animals to have multiple births, for human beings to do so is viewed as abnormal and hence a bad omen. Twins and triplets were either killed or abandoned. In the community, rituals of cleansing and propitiation were performed in order to avert the danger signalled by such births.

This attitude and the resulting acts deny the message of the dictum; they prevent the new borns from being the "I am" in order for the "we are" to continue. Such societies value communal safety more than an individual, in this case, the babies. In other cases, only a responsible adult——sorcerer, a murderer, adulterer or any one who commits a heinous offense——would be thought to threaten the safety and well-being of the community.

Ethically, it seems that operating here are two independent but not contradictory principles: The principles are life and death. In some societies multiple births are an affirmation of life, like having a bumper crop. In other societies, it is not the increase in itself, but the abnormality that signals danger, either death or some dreadful event, for the whole clan or community. A life (two in the case of twins) must be sacrificed for the survival of the community. Mbiti cautions that we need not react to such seemingly negative and callous practices emotionally because some rationale lies behind them, whether we can agree with the rationale or not. Multiple births may be a sign of blessing and hence harmony or of danger and hence of disharmony.

Mbiti states that the birth of a child is the concern of the whole community, living or dead. Among the Gikuyu of Kenya the parents put wristlets of goat's skin on the child. This rite symbolizes the bond between the child and the entire nation. The wristlet stands for what many African societies believe about the birth of a child, namely, that it continues the long chain of life going back to the Zamani, linking generations of humanity and also the Zamani with the Sasa. To Mbiti each generation is a wristlet, a sacred link in the chain of human existence that must never be broken. Therefore, birth brings with it communal obligations that one must grow to fulfill.

Western Christianity has neither provided an alternative theology of child-birth for African Christians, nor has it appropriated African socio-religious perceptions of birth. Thus African Christians keep floating between two worlds into which they are initiated.

3. *Naming*

Naming has to do with the concretizing of humanness as personal identity. It is giving visibility to the "I am" as the individuation of "we are." Mbiti tells us that among the Akamba people, the naming ceremony is very significant for both the child and the community. The Kikamba word for the naming ceremony, is *kuimithya*, meaning, humanization.[24] According to Mbiti, in receiving a name, the child is formally accepted, acknowledged to be essentially a human being, and regarded henceforth a member of the human community. Before this occasion, the child is an IT. Therefore, the beginning of the humanization process has to involve the investure of humanhood on to the child by the community. Naming is more than simply giving an identity label.

In many African cultures, one of the names given has to be a of one of the forebears living or dead. At times, the names have to do with some event, time, or wish. In this way, the naming and the names may have historical, phenomenological and ontological significance.[25] The danger to humanness lies in the threat of returning to existence as an IT instead of growing to become a full-fledged human being. Only full and responsible humanity can share in cosmic harmony. Once a name is given, one is made ready to enter into the world. Mbiti suggests that it would be most appropriate to link infant baptism to the naming ceremonies for African Christians.

4. *Initiation*

This important stage is most crucial to an individual. Initiation dramatizes the conflict between life and death and the desire for life to triumph for the good of cosmic harmony. It is an educational and moral program for children on the threshold of adulthood. It is a conferment of social status that places individuals within the social structures in the hope that they will make a contribution to social harmony. Therefore, to undergo initiation rites is ritually to encounter death and all its forces and to triumph over it.

Initiation as a major rite of passage is practiced in many African societies. Mbiti underscores its significance when he states: "The initiation of the young is one of the key moments in the rhythm of the individual life, which is also the rhythm of the corporate group of which the individual is a part. What happens to the single youth happens corporately to the parents, the relatives, the neighbors and the living-dead."[26] This initiation process not only forms a valuable social bond, but also spiritually cements the person and the community to other beings in the cosmos. As such, initiation has a crucial function in the realization and maintenance of cosmic harmony. It is important that these social and spiritual cosmic functions be articulated clearly. Western Christianity condemned some of initiation rites because of the ways they were carried out without any regard for the philosophy underlying them.

In order to establish African Christian thought on a more valid cultural foundation, Mbiti identifies the following as the underlying principles behind the act of initiation:

(a) The initiation process serves as an important transitional point
in the life of an individual from the more passive and dependent
stage of childhood to the more active and independent stage of
adulthood.

(b) It ritually introduces youth to the art of communal living and
commitment to its well-being. The act of withdrawing from society
for the duration of the ceremony symbolizes a process of dying,
living in the spirit world [27] and being reborn.

(c) It introduces the initiate to norms of adult life, responsibility
and accountability.

(d) It is educational because the youth are initiated into societal
values, appropriate behavior and given sexual education.

(e) It provides a means of establishing a mystical bond with the
living dead and with each other. The young who have been
initiated together become mystically and ritually bound to each
other for the rest of their life. In effect, they become one body,
one group,one community and one people.[28]

The parallels between this rite to the biblical symbolism of baptism
as a dying and a rising with Christ is obvious and close. Yet, in
many African countries, Western Christianity was adamantly
opposed to such rites because they were thought to be demonic,
especially when masks were used in the dances to celebrate the

occasion. The contrast between initiation in African culture and baptism/confirmation in Christianity is that the African rite is embedded within the humanizing process, while Christian rites are received apart from one's culture and are presented in an idiom that is not indigenous. As such, they are strangers to one's lived experience. It seems not to have occurred to representatives of Western Christianity that by rejecting these African rites so rich and deep in their spirituality, they were rejecting a people's sense of wholeness.

In societies where circumcision or clitoridectomy is part of the ritual, Mbiti says that the cut on the sex organs indicates the sacredness of sex in the sight of God, the spirits, the living dead, and human community. The sacredness is especially evident where the ceremonies are performed upon candidates who are reaching puberty. In this flowering stage, they need to be properly prepared for the time of their fruitful production, which is considered to be their reason for being. They are born to reproduce, that is, to perpetuate themselves, their clans and community. The whole community participates physically and mystically in the initiation process, and in so doing, is renewed. The initiation rites are performed to re-establish and confirm the human integrity of the initiates and the whole community before God and the spirit beings.

To remain uninitiated is to remain perpetually a child, regardless of one's physical age. It is to refuse to grow and to live up to one's mission and destiny as a human being. It is to remain uneducated about the knowledge of adult life. Throughout one's life, an uninitiated person is treated as immature and is denied all participation in the significant responsibilities that are the preserve and privilege of adults. Children from Christian homes who were denied this communitarian life-affirming process because the missionaries had declared it an evil and pagan practice suffered unimaginable traumas.[29] For Mbiti, the upholding of these rites and practices as significant aspects of African culture does not mean that he is unaware of some of the abuses, for instance, beatings and other hardships, inflicted on the initiates as part of the discipline. In the case of clitoridectomy, the mutilation can cause severe damage not only to the physical function of the genetalia but to sexual responses as well. Mbiti is only pointing to the positive contribution of these rites towards the realization of harmony and wholesomeness in the community.

5. *Marriage and Procreation*

An initiation ceremony that takes place when one reaches puberty is a preparation for marriage as the next rite of passage. In many societies, marriage, especially for girls, follows soon after the initiation rites have been accomplished. Actually, initiation is the badge of readiness and eligibility for marriage. Mbiti asserts, "For the African peoples, marriage is the focus of existence. It is the point where all the members of a given community meet: the departed, the living and those yet to be born. All dimensions of time meet here, and the whole drama of history is repeated, renewed and revitalized."[30] Mbiti rightly describes marriage as the focal point, the chief end of human existence. In addition, like other rites of passage, marriage clearly manifests a cosmic dimension. Marriage is one of the greatest fulfillments that one can have in African society. To be denied the opportunity to be fulfilled sexually and reproductively is to suffer human indignity of the first order.[31] Marriage is not an end in itself. The purpose of marriage is not simply sexual fulfillment, but rather to have children, which is a kind of self-fulfillment. The birth of children is the crown of one's human mission and hence one's humanity. In this connection, Mbiti states, "To be productive, in terms of having children, is one of the essential attributes of being a mature human being. The more productive a person is, the more he contributes to the society at large."[32] Marriage and procreation cannot be separated in African society, and without procreation there is virtually no marriage. Mbiti sees in procreation the reversal of the lost gift of immortality. As we will see later, this immortality is collective as well as personal. To choose not to marry is to rob the community of the opportunity to perpetuate itself and to deny oneself the top-most human prize, that of continued participation in an historical immortality. In some cases, Mbiti reports, one risks being called "sub-human," socially, at least. The understanding of personal dignity involves going through the humanizing processes and behaving accordingly as a human being, and one's ability to marry and have children is one such obligation. Although single persons are not socially ostracized, honor and recognition is grudgingly given to them. They are often despised and become the subjects of gossip and taunt songs. To choose not to marry is to disrupt the life chain of one's clan and a failure to fulfil one's obligation to it.

Given such instances of failure to be human Mbiti insists on the primary identity with Christ for the Christian. He recognizes that in some of these traditional beliefs, the freedom that is supposed to constitute our humanity is sacrificed on the communal altar of self-perpetuation, leaving no room for other life-styles. As

in some cases of multiple births, in marriage, singleness is deemed
abnormal because it is not in step with the community's norm and,
therefore, a deficit to the community. To such people, Jesus
becomes liberator because he releases them from the
marginalization and humiliation to which they are subjected and
makes them subjects of his mission.

Mbiti identifies two practices related to contracting
marriages in Africa that are the most misunderstood. The first is
the gifts given in exchange for the bride. This practice, Mbiti
thinks, has been wrongly called "bride-price." Local terms for it
do not bear that meaning.   The abuses of the custom
notwithstanding, the terms used in African languages do not
connote a commercial transaction. Since marriage is a communal
affair rather than a matter between two individuals, the gifts are
from the bridegroom's family to that of the bride. Mbiti explains
the significance of the gifts:

> The gift elevates the value attached to her as a
> person and as a wife. The gift legalizes her value
> and the marriage contract. The institution of this
> practice is the most concrete symbol of the marriage
> covenant and security. Under no circumstance the
> custom is a form of "payment", as outsiders have
> often mistakenly said.[33]

Mbiti obviously regards this tradition as related to the value of
being human and the concomitant social standing that is supposed
to go with it, not economic value. In my opinion, the abuse of
this custom renders marriage virtually a commercial transaction
where daughters are traded by fathers, brothers, and uncles, with
mothers, sisters, and aunts as accomplices. To those who pay, the

women are regarded as property; and that attitude can, and does
sometimes lead to very oppressive and dehumanizing practices in
both monogamous and polygamous relationships. The women are
trapped by the greed of their fathers and brothers for wealth on the
one hand and by the power of their husbands on the other. Since
procreation has such a high premium, mothers too are often
instrumental in arranging early marriages for their daughters. It
seems that the collusion of patriarchy, capitalism, the desire for
immortality, and all these compounded by personal sin,   are
factors behind abuses of marriage covenants.

Polygamy or polygyny is another practice that was
condemned by Western Christianity as immoral, undignified, and
an outrageous exploitation of women. Again without judging the
morality of the practice, Mbiti seeks the thinking behind the
practice. Again also most missionary agencies failed to look for
this underlying significance and thereby showed no appreciation
for this form of marriage. Mbiti enumerates the positive elements
in a polygamous arrangement. First, children are the glory of a
marriage; therefore, the more there are, the greater the glory of
the parents, especially the man. Second, economic reasons are a
factor in contracting polygamous relationships. Third, this
arrangement provides an opportunity for most people to have
some form of marriage relationship socially accepted as dignifying.
As a consequence, there were no "old maids" in African societies.
This does not mean that polygamous relationships are always
happy or successful, nor are they always miserable as many seem
to think. Among African peoples both monogyny and polygyny are
normal, legal, and socially approved marriage arrangements. Since
the missionaries assumed that they had come to work among

pagans, they were already prejudiced against such practices, which they interpreted as the very signs of paganism, in spite the fact that some leading biblical personalities were guilty of the same. Monogamy, the Christian norm, was good; polygamy was just the opposite: bad and entirely sinful. Mbiti rejects this attitude as unhelpful and based on flimsy biblical support. For Mbiti a theology that is not properly based on the Bible is a danger both to the Gospel as well as to the believing community.

According to Mbiti, the positive aspect of polygamy is that it helps to prevent or reduce unfaithfulness and prostitution. However, the practice is still being questioned, especially in regard to the dignity of women. It seems that polygamy is at best an exploitation of women's sexuality and labor. Mbiti does not discuss the rights and wrongs of polygamy. He explains, "I am simply presenting the facts and attempting to appreciate the thinking and experience of those involved in polygamous situations."[34]

Mbiti acknowledges the problems in polygamous relationships: quarrels and fights among wives and their children; the neglect of many wives by husbands as later wives are added; the burdens of clothing, feeding, and educating the many children; and the failure to bring up the children properly, which often results in undisciplined and difficult children. Mbiti, nevertheless, points out that problems of polygamous marriages are human problems and are not necessarily created by polygamy as such; the problems have been neither solved nor avoided by monogamous relationships. It is too simplistic to view monogamy and polygamy as ethical opposites and to judge polygamy/-gny on isolated negative incidents. Despite the problems and abuses that occur in marriage, Mbiti maintains that for African peoples marriage is a "sacred drama in which everyone is a religious participant," and in that light of changed economic, social, and religious conditions, "polygamy is becoming increasingly unworkable, outdated and a social deficit."[35] It is to be noted that Mbiti does not condemn polygamy on biblical grounds.

In relation to the concept of time, Mbiti maintains that marriage and procreation are a stage of life that points towards the Zamani. Many women keep on having babies until they can have them no more. And as long as men are sexually active, they will continue to have children. Of course, different customs govern when a woman may stop bearing.[36] Mbiti reminds us that bearing children not only fulfills one's manhood and womanhood, and therefore one's potential humanity, but also maintains the ancestral line. He explains: "To be presupposes making it possible for others also to be when one is and has been. The we are who will be, can only be because I am, just as I am because others have been."[37] For Mbiti, marriage is a crucial ontological juncture indeed. It is a celebration of life and the meeting of the past and present generations.

6. *Death and Destiny*

For all practical purposes, historical existence ends at death because, as Mbiti states, death stands between the world of human beings and the world of the spirits, between the visible and the invisible.[38] Strictly speaking, the process of becoming human in Africa would end at this point, were it not for the sense of life beyond the grave, which is conceived of anthropomorphically. This sense of life beyond the grave has also serious implications for life in historical time. Life beyond the grave is the real human destiny understood as *telos*.[39] Procreation might be the sacred duty that one must fulfil, to use Mbiti's phrase, but the spirit world is the sacred destiny that no one misses.

Mbiti points out that apart from mythic explanations of the original cause of death as a permanent reality, personal death is accounted for variously, for instance, by magic, sorcery, and witchcraft. Many African peoples usually associate personal death with some human agency. Rarely do people die a "natural" death. Death is, more often than not, attributed to some human being who possesses an evil heart or eye. The cause of death may be attributed to the living-dead, especially when they have been neglected, their mortuary ritual has not been performed satisfactorily, or they suffered some violent death themselves which leaves them disgruntled, angry, and bent on revenge. Sometimes death is considered an act of God, especially when it is due to some natural phenomenon, for instance, lightning, but, more often than not, lightning itself is attributed to human agency. One's death can be good or bad. A bad death results in disharmony for both the deceased and the living community, while a good death ensures harmony between the community and the living-dead.

Therefore, death is viewed as both natural and unnatural. It is natural because its occurrence is due to some mishap in mythical time or because God causes it. It is unnatural because humanity was not created for death, but for immortality. Even though death is accepted, the acceptance comes as it were, under protest. The hope for immortality is not quenched by death. The belief in an after-life is very strong in many African societies.

Mbiti tells us that death is a departure and not a complete annihilation of a person.[40] It is a radical human transformation from historical to spiritual existence. Death is a personal and helpless encounter with a human phenomenon that immobilizes life itself and transforms human existence to spirited existence. The belief in the spirit-life does not give comfort to the living because, as Mbiti tells us, "death is painful, it is terrorizing, it is tormenting and grievous."[41] It deeply disrupts the pattern of kinship relationships, thereby bringing disharmony to life's rhythm.

Mbiti thinks that elaborate funeral rituals are ways of keeping alive the presence of the deceased among the living. This remembering turns death into a slow process of moving from the Sasa to the Zamani. He writes,

> At the moment of physical death the person becomes a living-dead: he is neither alive physically, nor dead relative to the corporate group. His own Sasa period is over, he enters fully into the Zamani period; but, as far as the living who knew him are concerned, he is kept "back" in the Sasa period, from which he can only disappear gradually. Those who have nobody to keep them in the Sasa period in reality "die" immediately, which is a great tragedy that must be avoided at all costs.[42]

For Mbiti, to be held in memory is far better than being an unknown and an undifferentiated spirit. He asserts further that when one ceases to be in the category of the living-dead, one loses one's name and human personality. The ontological destiny is to lose one's humanness in order to gain full spiritness.[43] One becomes an "IT" again.

If, as Mbiti puts it, death is the end of the real and complete humanity, what has death and the hereafter got to do with the fact of being human? Death is a salutary reminder of human frailty. This deep sense of vulnerability in a capricious universe has led to the establishment of elaborate belief and ritual systems aimed at securing the lost, and yet profoundly missed, initial cosmic harmony. People in many parts of Africa are under a constant threat of obliteration by famine, sickness, murders, and moral pollution. Therefore, to be human is constantly to face this threat. Under this threat of death, the ontological desire not only to live long and well but to live forever is intensified. Therefore, salvation is directed at countering the threats of death, increasing one's life installments, and achieving personal and communal well-being and immortality through the reproductive processes. The humanizing process partly prepares people to avoid being agents of this force; instead, it teaches them to affirm life and harmony by struggling against all forces of death. Mbiti thinks that the means African religion has provided to deal with this human predicament are inadequate: "But there are no salvatory myths to remove man from death or to cancel death from human life. Man has learned to live with death... Man conquers death on a corporate basis even if death conquers him on a personal level."[44] The corporate conquest is achieved through the reproductive processes. It perpetuates the human race but not the individual person.

Humanity and Evil

The problem of evil is presupposed in the humanization process and is foundational to it in a negative way. The process of humanization implies the negation of evil because evil runs counter to humanness. Since evil is a significant aspect of our human experience in the quest for cosmic harmony, it deserves separate discussion. It is ironic that in the African view even though human beings were alienated from God by foolish and inconsiderate action, when it comes to personal evil, God does not enter the picture. Historically, evil is a local affair limited to horizontal relationships. The equivalent of this confession made to God, "Against you, you *only*, have I sinned and done what is evil in your sight,"[45] does not exist on a personal level for Africans. Mbiti is concerned that unless this way of thinking is understood and taken into account in interpreting Christian teaching on sin, African Christian eventual conception of sin or evil will be a distorted one. The African Christian will limit it only to one relationship at the expense of the other. The relational connectedness will remain incomplete.

Mbiti asserts that for many African societies, an act is evil because it is punished and rather than punished because it is evil. Morality based on tradition has no direct relation to God even though, as Mbiti states, God is acknowledged as the final guardian of law and order and of the moral and ethical codes. God created moral beings and the exercise of morality is within the human domain. Morality among African peoples is not derived from an equivalent of the Decalogue given on some sacred mountain but rather through a "humanity based" culture,[46] which Mbiti acknowledges is also God's medium of self-revelation. Here again, we see the radical separation between God's domain and that of human beings. The exercise of morality is a human privilege. By asserting that God is still regarded as the guardian of morality,

Mbiti avoids implications of a deistic position in which God has left the world to itself. Such deism does not belong to African traditional religions, in which God is acknowledged as present to the community of the living, living-dead, and spirits.

Mbiti notes a paradox when it comes to moral praxis. The corporate nature of society and its strong kinship ties leave much moral action to be desired. He observes that instead of providing a preponderance of virtue, a real mix of virtue and vice exists in African societies. Like the parabolic field, wheat and tares are left to grow together.[47] Mbiti finds some comfort in that African societies are not the only ones to face this condition. The condition is universal and human. To illustrate this, he points out certain national dispositional proclivities.

> By nature, Africans are neither angels nor demons; they possess and exercise the potentialities of both angels and demons. They can be as kind as the Germans, but they can be as murderous as the Germans; Africans can be as generous as the Americans, but they can be as greedy as the Americans; they can be as friendly as the Russians, but they can be as cruel as the Russians; they can be as honest as the English, but they can be equally hypocritical. In their human nature Africans are Germans, Swiss, Chinese, Indians or English——they are men.[48]

Evil is simply a human problem. Mbiti mentions these nationalities not because they are the standard bearers of morality, but because people from Europe and America believed that they were morally better than the so-called pagan and primitive Africans. Mbiti is, therefore, simply pointing out that in actual fact, they have no claim whatsoever to moral superiority. The reality of human existence is one of moral contradiction; there are no exceptions.

Mbiti finds African morality to be a morality of conduct rather than of being. However, Mbiti is obviously unhappy with this particular dichotomy. He asserts that what one does also defines what one is, rather than what one is defining what one does.[49] But on neither counts does Mbiti find the doctrine of Original sin in African traditional religions. One is a sinner because one has committed the actual sin. Then he goes on to declare, ". . . we must emphasize that in African religion they do not speak of moral estrangement between God and man. . . . The question of original sin is, therefore, out of place.[50] The process of humanization is aimed at nurturing people so that they do not commit evil; thus communal harmony will be maximized. The emphasis on the difference between God and human beings falls more on the ontological quality than on moral purity. Therefore, morality is not primarily a matter of spiritual conformity or breach of moral law but has to do with the increase or decrease of human integrity and harmony.

Humanity and Salvation

According to Mbiti, salvation in the African religious traditions has a different focus from the Christian view. Salvation in African traditional religion is concerned with, "...physical and immediate dangers (of individual and more often of the community). ...Salvation is not just an abstraction; it is concrete, told in terms of both what has happened and is likely to be encountered by people as they go through daily experience."[51] In keeping with his concept of time, Mbiti maintains that in

traditional religions salvation is either a past or a present event. He
asserts emphatically that the issue of eschatological salvation does
not arise because Africans' thinking does not accommodate any
eschatological view of time. We noted in the previous chapter that
Mbiti was critical of the missionary preaching on eschatology
because it cast the benefits of salvation from the present to the
future. Mbiti contends that salvation is a present experience and
that its eschatological aspects make sense only in light of God's
eternal Now. Therefore, the African desire to experience salvation
as a present reality fits into the biblical emphasis of an
eschatology that is realized but not yet consummated.

For Mbiti, the African view of salvation differs from the
biblical view because it has nothing to do with sin.[52] It is not
salvation from sin that people worry about, even though they do
seek salvation or rescue from the consequences of evil. Since
African religion is not primarily based on being lost spiritually,
spiritual redemption is not its focus. Mbiti confirms this by saying,

> ... the question of salvation from moral evil is also
> out of question. African religion, in this respect,
> did not produce the concept of spiritual redemption
> or salvation... That cosmic outreach of salvation is
> unknown and would be impossible within the
> context of African religious heritage.[53]

Apart from the normal running of the cosmos in its varied
rhythmic patterns and with all its life forces, there is no offer of
cosmic salvation within African traditional practice. Mbiti states,

> Man just accepted the situation as it turned out to
> be, and has lived with it since then. Through

prayers, sacrifices and offerings, man still
approaches God, and God provides for man's needs
in various ways. Through marriage and procreation,
man fights against death, thereby keeping death
under some measure of control.[54]

Since time has no future dimension, there can be no future hope.
The only hope, apart from having children to carry one's memory,
is to die and move back into the Zamani. If salvation means the
realization of human integrity and harmony, wholeness, and well-
being, then Mbiti thinks that it cannot be realized in traditional
religion because of: the lack of an eschatological future dimension
of time; the fact of death; and an absence of sin as the most
fundamental dislocation in human and cosmic harmony. He finds
all attempts at bringing about full salvation inadequate. Therefore
the quest for cosmic harmony remains unfulfilled.

Humanity and the Cosmos

Mbiti tells us that the embodiment of the physical and
spiritual in the one human body and the possession of a moral
consciousness qualify human beings for a priestly role in relation
to God and on behalf of all creation.[55] Human beings are fitted
for this role because they link God to nature and nature to God by
their ontological place in the cosmos. Being related to nature,
people communicate with nature by personifing it so that they can
solicit its help. The personification of nature underscores the fact
that human beings are participants in and are not outside or above
nature. Personification expresses the ontological relatedness of the
cosmos. People seek harmony with nature for their own well-being
as well as nature's. European thought has generally called such

practices animism. Mbiti rejects this nomenclature as inappropriate; it is based on faulty understanding of African religious practices.

Mbiti says that prayer in the African religious traditions is theologically revealing, showing how human beings understand themselves. Prayers provide "a spiritual picture of man painted by himself while posing at a religious moment."[56] Mbiti finds a prayer from the Didinga of the Sudan appropriately illustrates how humanity as priest solicits the kindness of nature and expresses respect towards it. He reminds us that behind the personification of nature lies "God, the creator and keeper of all things." The prayer is recited by "the Warden of the Forest" in the presence of God, the living, the departed, and the whole earth. In part the prayer runs:

> O Earth, wherever it be my people dig, be kindly to
> them. Be fertile when they give the little seeds to
> your keeping. Let your generous warmth nourish
> them and your abundant moisture germinate them.
> Let them swell and sprout, drawing life from you,
> and burgeon under your fostering care . . .
>
> O trees of the forest and glades, fall easily under
> the axe. Be gentle to my people. . . . Break no
> limb in your anger. Crush no one in your
> displeasure . . .
> Conspire together, O Earth and rivers, conspire
> together O Earth and rivers and forests. Be gentle
> and give us of your teeming plenty . . .[57]

Through prayer, ritual, and sacrifices, humanity interacts with the world in very personal ways while at the same time, interacting with God. Mbiti says that humanity belongs to both the physical and the spiritual worlds, the visible as well as the invisible worlds. Humanity has a role in the interaction of these two worlds. Part of that role is to contribute to the   maintenance of the cosmic harmony.

It is at prayer that spiritual values are made most manifest. There is a marked emphasis on purity, cleanliness of heart, and holiness; the humility of human beings before God and other spiritual beings; trust, love, peace; sorrow at the thought that God has abandoned them; and praise and thanksgiving for blessings received. Human beings expect to maintain vital relationships with other beings in the cosmos. It is, therefore, in its priestly role that the spiritual dimension of humanity becomes manifest. However, this role is not independent of other human concerns.

One notices in the African conception of humanity's priestly role some semblance to the Reformation doctrine of the priesthood of all believers and the Pauline association of the salvation of human beings with the salvation of all creation.[58] One can understand Mbiti's frustration and even anger that against western Christianity for consigning such a rich religious heritage to hell along with its myriad practitioners. Such condemnations were an affront to God in whose name they were being issued because, as Mbiti claims, God was there before the missionaries came. Therefore, no African theology can develop and deserve the titles African and theology that does not seriously seek to take this religious heritage into account. Mbiti contends that Christianity in Africa owes its success largely to this rich African religiosity, which was prepared by the Holy Spirit to receive the Gospel that in turn fulfills it.

In spite of this noble role of humanity as the ontological juncture and as nature's priest, worship in African traditional religion is more utilitarian than spiritual, Mbiti tells us. Even though God is presupposed all the time, God's glory is not of immediate concern. Mbiti may be closer to the truth when he suggests that God is seen as being at the disposal of human beings. Their major concern is humanity's well-being which serves also as one of the indicator of cosmic harmony.

Mbiti sees some inadequacies in all that the African people do to keep the cosmic harmony whole. The inadequacies that Mbiti identifies, do not disqualify African religiosity from being a suitable preparation for the Gospel, much less consign it to the devil. However, the greater cosmic human vision of peace, harmony and well-being remains elusive, especially in the face of rapid changes taking place in the last two centuries, to which we must now turn.

CHAPTER FIVE

AFRICAN HUMANITY AND WESTERN IMPACT:
Dilemma of Change and Modernity

Mbiti has identified history as one of the sources for doing theology in Africa. In Chapter Two, we saw why Mbiti considers historical consciousness as basic to a people's self- understanding. Mbiti has divided African history into three phases and says that each has left its imprint on the life of the church.[1] The three historical phases are: first, the long history of African peoples, the aspects of this were discussed in Chapters Two and Three. Second, the period of European intrusion and colonial rule which led to the subdivision of the continent, the creation of new countries, and ended in African struggles for political liberation. The third phase is that of independent nationhood. We will focus on the second phase, of which Mbiti says: "This phase ranges in length from a few decades to several centuries of foreign rule. It paved, even if painfully sometimes, the way for modern national consciousness."[2] In this chapter, I will attempt to show how, according to Mbiti, the changes precipitated by European presence, resulting very often in painful experiences for Africans, have shaped their sense of humanity.

European Intrusion

European intrusion into the African continent for more than four centuries precipitated a great human crisis because the invasion of European power and culture was both pervasive and brutal. Mbiti describes this catastrophic situation for African humanity under the rubric "Changing Man and His Problems." Change is inevitable, but not every change is beneficial to everyone. The pertinent question is, What has this revolutionary change meant for African people and their sense of being human in the world? This question should be kept in the forefront of our minds in this chapter. African humanity was caught unawares in this change, which Mbiti characterizes as rapid, radical, and total.[3] Europeans aimed at either superimposing a Euro-centric worldview onto the African worldview or simply eradicating the latter altogether.

Although Europe first entered Africa in the fifteenth century, it was not until towards the end of the nineteenth century that change started to take on revolutionary proportions. Mbiti states: ". . . the changes are total, involving the whole existence of the African peoples, and making their impact upon the religious, economic, political as well as social life."[4] These changes were part of a world revolution. As Mbiti puts it, they were in essence aimed at, "a revolution of man as a whole," as far as African humanity was concerned. African people were to be transformed into the cultural image of the colonial overlords and ladies. Mbiti describes the nature of this effort by the Europeans:

> Europe began to transform Africa and if possible to make it resemble itself in many respects. Even European names were substituted for African and religious names of local places and individuals. Mini Englands, mini Germanies, mini Frances and mini Italies, were being planted everywhere on *our* [my emphasis] continent. Europe had divided up Africa, Europe meant to rule Africa and Europe began to change Africa.[5]

This revolution took Africans by surprise and by storm. The

African people were not prepared for it, since they did not seek it nor were they asked permission for its implementation. Europe imposed itself on them by force of arms, duplicity, threats, and empty treaties not worthy of the paper they were signed on. The changes brought a new rhythm, so that it was imperative that, as Mbiti states, "the man of Africa must get up and dance, for better or for worse, on the stage of world drama,"[6] Who ever controls the rhythm controls the form of the dance, and Africans have been dancing ever since to a foreign tune. How has this foreign tune affected their humanity?

Mbiti charges that the new rhythm disrupted the African image and universe. It forced Africans to move from personal, "tribal" humanity to an impersonal, universal humanity. This fundamental dislocation called into question their sense of place in the world. Furthermore, as if domination itself was not enough, attempts were being made to incorporate them into a universal humanity, which actually was Europeanism universalized. In the process African peoples had their persons subjected to subhuman treatment. Often demonic, the rhythm was bound to produce havoc, and it did.

Form and Change

Mbiti notes that this revolutionary onslaught to dominate and change the African people moved in a three-pronged advance. The prongs were different, but interrelated, namely, western Christianity, western political imperialism, and capitalism. These forms of domination tended to aid one another in exerting a tight multiple grip on the life and culture of African people. In his appeal to his compatriots, David Livingstone, renowned missionary explorer, illustrates this close connection between commercial and religious interests.

> I beg to direct your attention to Africa; --I know that in a few years I shall be cut off in that country, which is now open; do not let it be shut again! I go back to Africa to try to make an open path for commerce and Christianity; do you carry out the work which I have begun. I LEAVE IT WITH YOU![7]

It has been observed that Livingstone did not put commerce before Christianity by accident; the order indicates what was primary in his mind and that of his audience. Throughout colonial history, more often than not, Christian expansion has followed very closely on the heels of commerce, while both served the political ends of the imperialistic nations. African people were now destined to be shaped by these three major forces that characterized the advance of the West.

1. *Western Christianity*

Mbiti has maintained that Christianity as a religion is indigenous to Africa, in view of its presence in north Africa from the first century and in Ethiopia since the fourth. The Western Christianity that reached most of sub-Saharan African in the nineteenth century was a second wave of Christianity. It is this type of Christianity that has created cultural and religious dilemmas for African people. Christianity announced a new way of living that challenged the African ways at some very critical points, thereby undermining the African worldview.

Though critical of some missionary methods and theology,

Mbiti has praised some missionaries for daring to bring the Gospel to Africa. He makes a plea that criticism of the evils of the missionary movements and imperialism, should not simply become a blanket accusation, but should include an appreciative assessment, because much was positive and genuine.[8]

Even though Christian missions have claimed that the Gospel was their primary concern, they included with it much cultural baggage, which was rarely subsumed under the demands of the Gospel. Mbiti considers that the nineteenth-century model of mission best exemplifies the cultural appeal as a missionary motive.[9] The cultural baggage included Western education, medicine, political institutions, economic opportunism, racial and cultural prejudice, and technology. As Mbiti points out:

> The gospel by its very nature is revolutionary, but Christianity in its modern return to Africa is the main carrier of all the elements of this world revolution. It is necessary to draw a distinction between the Gospel and Christianity which are not synonymous at certain points.[10]

Mbiti rightly recognizes that mission Christianity was in itself a revolutionary force, it aimed to revolutionize African people, starting with their being and their entire world outlook. Missionaries became agents of this revolution through the institutions that they established, such as schools, commercial enterprises, and hospitals, and by being accomplices in the establishment of colonialism. Through these structures, they expected to win not only a hearing for the Gospel in the "pagan" communities, but also to convert the heathen to Western ways of thinking. The revolution was to affect the whole person.

Mbiti states that, in outline, the Gospel message of the missionaries was that Africans were made in God's image and likeness as was the rest of humankind, that they too had fallen in sin and were still in sin, that Jesus came into the world to save sinners and to bring them to heaven, that the world would come to an end when God would judge humankind, and that only those who believe in Jesus were assured a place with God forever while the rest would be thrown into eternal fire. This truth in the context of Western civilization, formed the total package, which was non-negotiable. This package was partly contained in the various catechisms that the new converts had to memorize and assimilate. To convert was not only to submit to Christ's Lordship, but also to accept the lordship of a Western cultural worldview. Although the Gospel's demand was orthopraxis, the missionary emphasis was on orthodoxy, an intellectual assent, as defined in their various confessions and taught in their catechisms, which followed a propositional model of pedagogy. Mbiti criticizes, for instance, the content of the African Inland Mission Catechism and hymnody because their teaching on eschatology which, as we saw in Chapter Two, has had a theologically disastrous effect on African Christians. Through the catechisms which they were told to memorize before they could be baptized, the confessions out of Europe's theological battles, and the trapping of Western technology and culture, the African converts were redefined. They began to understand themselves in a new way. Because this new understanding was to a large extent racially and culturally antagonistic to most of what they knew themselves to be as human beings, it precipitated for many an existential crisis. Suddenly they became people of two worlds at war with each other. They also discovered that within Christianity itself, the various schools of theological thought and traditions were engaged in theological warfare that began to affect relationships between communities.

2. *Political Imperialism*

At the Berlin Conference of 1884, European nations agreed to partition Africa among themselves. Mbiti explains that for Africans this act of partition meant:

> . . . the arrival of European settlers, businessmen, gold and diamond diggers, colonial administrators, the founding of new cities, the construction of railway roads, the introduction of new laws and new economic system. [11]

These undertakings took a tremendous human toll on Africa. Since Africa and the Africans were now the property of Europe, the European long-term goal was to transform most of Africa and most Africans as far as possible into the image of Europe for the benefit and comfort of Europeans. The Africans were to satisfy themselves with the crumbs that fell from the imperial masters' and mistresses' table. Therefore, large tracts of hunting and grazing grounds and cultivated lands were appropriated, which deprived Africans of the one element that both gave them a sense of rootedness and belonging in the world, and made economic survival possible. The seizure of land was tantamount to sentencing many to death.

Mbiti has rightly observed that the African peoples' response to European encroachment has been one of ever-increasing acts of defiance and resistance, which from time to time broke out into open conflict as their sense of being human in the world was reduced to servitude. Their only crime was the color of their skin and, secondarily, technological and military weakness. In almost all cases of violent confrontation, resistance was met with brutal force, resulting in great human loss.[12] Mbiti captures for us the consequences of these rebellions upon the African people:

> In some parts Africans tried to resist but were overcome by Europeans who slaughtered them like beasts, who burnt down their villages, who put men and women into prisons, who forced them to quit their lands and become laborers in European farms or "house-boys" for European masters and mistresses. The new change started and continued in blood and tears, in suppression and humiliation, through honest and dishonest means, by consent and by force, by choice and by subjugation. . . . Africa had paid heavily for the change which originated outside and was initially being forced upon her.[13]

This colonial take-over was in itself a transformation of the long distant, cross-Atlantic slavery into a local "domestic" servitude, which was no more civilized and humane in most respects than the former, itself in disrepute and decline in the late nineteenth century. It was slave trade brought home to roost. Therefore, politically, the Africans experienced overwhelming changes in power relations and structures, in both of which they were greatly disadvantaged. This affected seriously the way they understood their humanity: They were forced to see themselves through the Western eyes as inferior, infantile, and beastly. No good treatment could cancel out this understanding, because it had become the most fundamental perception. And good treatment was more the exception than the rule as long as foreigners were politically in control. It has been observed that there was a paradox involved in the European treatment of Africans: A capacity to do them great good, and to inflict the worsed evil.

3. *Capitalism*

True to his general approach, Mbiti does not provide an economic and social analysis of capitalism but rather describes it phenomenologically as a factor of change:

> A primary money economy has been introduced to Africa. It is making its force felt even in the remotest parts of the continent. People grow cash crops like cocoa, coffee, tea, cotton and tobacco. Others work for money in all sorts of employment. This new economy introduces the concept of time as a commodity to be sold and bought; it involves also earning and spending money with all the dangers, temptation, difficulties and risks that go with it.[14]

Mbiti is keenly aware that capitalism has an ugly inhuman face. He actually classifies capitalism as an anti-religious movement on the same level as communism and secularism, especially when "it exploits man to such a degree that he becomes simply a tool or robot and loses his humanity." Contrary to Marx, however, Mbiti sees the inhumanity of capitalism as not inherent, but as a tendency. It is the materialist tendency of capitalism that is anti-human; that is the tendency to view human beings as having only material needs. This tendency to playdown human spiritual needs runs counter to the African traditional view of humanity, which considers human beings to be both physical and spiritual.[15] Mbiti thinks that capitalism and other -isms can be made serviceable to human beings by appropriating them into Christianity in order to provide them with a religious dimension. If this is not done, humanity is bound to be in subjection to them.

These three aspects of European presence were the most crucial factors in bringing about the revolutionary changes that were to affect the African people so radically. While each aspect had its own inner dynamism, racial and cultural factors unified them into a mighty racial torrent destructive of all other understandings of being human. For Mbiti, this racial and cultural onslaught had mixed blessings for the Africans; it brought some changes that were beneficial in spite of its brutalities. Our interest is to see how the African sense of being human was affected by the benefits and brutalities. Furthermore, by relating to African philosophy and religion, Mbiti implies that no African theology would be adequate that did not take it into account. Nor would any African Christian anthropology be relevant that did not relate to this experience.

The Effect of Change on African Humanity

Mbiti maintains that the European interlude has had both negative and positive consequences. Negatively, it caused the "detribalization" of people as they left their villages in search of employment. The foundations of "tribal" life, namely, extended family, kinship, community, and language were undermined. The ontological sense of being rooted and related was also shaken. This shaking of the foundations of the African peoples' ontological sense, was especially felt when Europeans began not only to define but to control the definition of one's being and place in the world. "Detribalization" is not simply a change of location, but a shift of consciousness from a tribal mind set to a Western mentality and from being a particular people to being a secondary extension of another people. Mbiti observes this impact on individuals:

> This sudden detachment from land to which Africans are mystically bound, and the thrust into situations where corporate existence has no meaning, have produced dehumanized individuals in the mines, industry and cities. The change means that the individuals are severed, cut off, pulled out and separated from corporate morality, customs and traditional solidarity. They have no firm roots any more. They are simply uprooted but not necessarily transplanted. They float in life like a cloud. They live as individuals, but they are dead to the corporate humanity of their forefathers.
> For the individual the change has come too suddenly, plunging him into a darkness for which he has not been traditionally prepared. . . . So he becomes an alien both to traditional life and the new life brought about by modern change.[16]

For someone whose self-consciousness is rooted in strong communal and kinship relations, the experience of this change is indeed dehumanizing especially when coupled with the poor living conditions that many experience in urban shanty towns and slums. If the physical conditions are dehumanizing, then the psychological disruptions and spiritual deprivations even more greatly undermine Africans' sense of being. The urban situations, which Africans did not create and which operates according to foreign rules, do not present a uniform system of social norms and customs for the African people but become an amalgam of many such norms, customs, languages and peoples. Such situations compound the disorientation for many Africans. Mbiti alludes to an important fact here: the physical and socio-economic infrastructures have a tremendous bearing on the definition of a people's existence and sense of being.

Worse still, for Mbiti, is the tension created by the perception of time in the two worldviews. The African worldview pulls Africans towards the *Zamani*, while the European view beckons them to the future. These two orientations are, according to Mbiti, "neither harmonious nor creative for the majority of Africans." However, the introduction of future hope is both a blessing and a curse. It is a blessing because it releases the Africans from being prisoners of the past so they can begin to dream dreams and work for their own progress. It is a curse because the discovery of a dynamic future dimension is dangerous. It becomes a source of instability when expectations are unfulfilled and eventually, the cause of illusion. The danger and the illusion, Mbiti argues, lie in the expectation that adopting the new ways would usher Africa into the joys of the West, as if the processes of adopting the new and of casting off the old ways were one and the same. Mbiti urges that only a responsible and responsive government that seeks the best for all its citizens can lead its people to the realization of their dreams; otherwise, the dreams turn into a nightmare.

Mbiti points out further that the colonial interlude rendered almost all the African people politically impotent. African political institutions were "destroyed, suppressed or modified. "People who had never been subjected to foreign rule," states Mbiti, "found themselves without political power."[17] Eventually, this lack of political power and the humiliation that accompanied it fueled the fires of resistance that eventually brought about decolonization.

African Struggle for Liberation

Mbiti has alluded to the fact that the African people did not always passively accept bad treatment.[18] With the passage of time, European colonial domination of Africa was met with increasing resistance. The legendary *Pax Britannica*, for instance, was maintained by use of brute force and at a great cost to the Africans, as Mbiti has indicated. While it diminished inter-ethnic conflict and created enlarged states, it drew Africans into European wars, more destructive and devastating than any Africans had ever experienced. After the wars they received no compensation and support for their contribution. Africans paid with their lives for the responsibility of governments in which they had no voice.

At stake, as Mbiti sees it, were Africans' humanity, their freedom to determine their destiny, and the loss of land as their primary means of economic production. All are important aspects in anyone's sense of being authentically human. Africans resented being treated as if they were either children or not human at all. They were forced to carry heavy loads for long distances for white people for little or no pay. It was not uncommon to see them used as transportation for white people and missionaries were no exception to this usage. By imposing taxes, European forced Africans to become cheap labor on their estates and business establishments, where they were deployed at back-breaking tasks.

Africans received the harshest punishments that could be meted out, as though they were animals. They were pushed off all good land and even turned into workers and tenants on their own land. All these evils told Africans that they were inferior in every way, a subhuman race. Their resistance to white oppression was fundamentally a rejection of this humiliating view. The resistance manifested itself in many forms.

Mbiti enables us to look at one form of this resistance against European presence when he describes the emergence of Independent Churches in Africa. The reasons he sees for this religious phenomenon also apply to the political and economic spheres. As factors responsible for sparking off separatism he lists: resentment of European rule and control, African nationalism or black solidarity, African leadership charisma and styles, the failure of Christianity to penetrate deeply into African religiosity, the need to come to terms with new forces which undermined the old foundations, and the hope of an immediate paradise to be realized soon.[19]

Africans resisted Colonialism on the physical level, while on the intellectual level they issued more and more increasing challenges. Africans began to see that the biblical claim that all human beings were made in the image of God was compromised by those who oppressed the black people, missionaries included. This biblical assertion became a frequent critical tool against black oppression. The political history and constitutional developments of the oppressors were turned against them. The African people felt the need to retrieve themselves from the European intellectual garbage dump where they had been culturally consigned.

For self-determination, Africans needed to get control of

the institutions that colonialists and imperialists employed to dominate and oppress. The humiliation that Africans had suffered, Mbiti points out, could not be swallowed indefinitely. Within two decades after the Second World War, almost all of Africa was politically liberated. Mbiti is fully aware that political liberation was an essential first step toward and condition for the realization of full and authentic humanity for black people. He is under no illusion that political independence was not to be the ultimate goal. Indeed, the journey toward the realization of authentic humanity was not going to be smooth sailing. Mbiti justifies his cautious assessment of future prospects for independent Africa by observing that African governments inherited colonial structures of government, that the forces of nationalism characterized by a multi-ethnic population were not easy to harmonize, and that the world context for African politics was dangerous, difficult, and foreign. As he put it, "The political pot in Africa is still bubbling, and great is the man who can stir it without getting smeared or even scorched."[20]   Political liberation is not, for Mbiti, the realization of authentic selfhood on both the personal and national level, but only one preliminary condition. Much more was necessary in order to create a climate in which authentic humanity could begin to develop and eventually flourish. Mbiti saw that Christianity, understood as the incarnate Gospel in terms of the mission of Jesus and not as manifested in Western Christianity, bears an awesome responsibility in bringing about this human development toward authentic selfhood.

To meet the challenge of this pervasive and revolutionary change, many ideological and theological attempts have sought to provide a new vision of humanity in black Africa. They attempt at taking charge of defining oneself as African peoples, and Mbiti looks at three of these: Negritude as presented by Leopold Sedar Senghor, African Personality as described by Ezekiel Mphahlele, and Black Theology as it manifested itself in USA and South Africa. Mbiti has weighed all three and found each wanting. The first two, Mbiti thinks, are attempts to recover the cultural Zamani. But because Africans' temporal orientation has changed since Christianity introduced a future dimension which is eschatological, these idealogies that look to the Zamani cannot usefully serve Africans in fulfilling their human destiny.

Negritude

The term Negritude was coined by the poet Aime' Ce'saire' of Martinique in the West Indies and popularized in Africa by Leopold Sedar Senghor, the late president of Senegal. Presented in the form of a philosophical and cultural ideology, it was a courageous attempt by Senghor to rationalize the meaning Africans perceive in their view of life and the world. In order to appreciate Mbiti's reaction to Negritude, it is important to see how Senghor defines it.

Senghor defines Negritude both negatively and positively. Negatively, he says: "it is not a defence of a skin and a color, not an attachment to a particular race, our own, although such an attachment is quite legitimate."[21] However, viewed positively, it is ". . .the awareness by a particular group or people of its own situation in the world, and the expression of it by means of concrete images."[22]

Negritude is being aware of one's identity and naming it with pride. For the sake of universality or fear of reverse racism,

Senghor expunges the color content from a color-coded word and defines Negritude so universally that one is left to wonder whether white persons could accept it as a view of their own self-awareness and pride. However, Senghor's heart is not in universality. He laments the Africans' situation, "Africa's misfortune has been that our secret enemies, in defending their values, have made us despise our own."[23] As a cultural aspect of African experience, Senghor describes Negritude as:

> . . .made of human warmth. It is democracy quickened by the sense of communion and brotherhood between men. More deeply in works of art, which are a people's most authentic expression of itself, it is sense of image and rhythm, sense of symbol and beauty.[24]

For Senghor, culture is living people, and artifacts are bathed in and reflect a people's humanity.

Senghor explains the historical and existential circumstances that gave birth to Negritude.

> In what circumstances did Aime Cesaire and I launch the word Negritude between 1933 and 1935? At that time, along with several other black students, we were plunged into a sort of panic-stricken despair. The horizon was blocked. No reform was in sight and the colonizers were justifying our political and economic dependence by the theory of the *tabula rasa*... . In order to establish an effective revolution, our revolution, we first had to divest ourselves of our borrowed attire——that of assimilation——and assert our being, that is to say our Negritude.[25]

Mbiti is very critical of this idealistic outlook on African culture. He sees it as elitist and of no relevance to the rural masses. His verdict is that:

> Negritude is... a comfortable exercise for the elite who wants, seeks and finds it when he looks at the African Zamani and hopes for an African future. It has neither dogma nor taboos, neither feast days or ceremonies... Negritude is because it is said to be. It is identified with the Negro Africans, but do Africans identify with Negritude? That is the dilemma of Negritude as an ideology.[26]

The tension that Mbiti feels in respect to the position of Senghor can be understood from two viewpoints. The first is Mbiti's aversion to the particularity of color implied in the term Negritude, despite Senghor's explicit universalism. As we will see below, he shows the same aversion to Black theology. The second point is that Mbiti does not seem to trust ideologies as sources of what is best for humanity. For him, ideologies tend to idealize historical situations instead of taking them as they are. The fact that Negritude has a foreign origin, even though it emerged out of black experience, makes it unacceptable to him. For Mbiti, the foundation of a truly African vision of humanity must emerge from Africa; it cannot depend on any foreign philosophical, ideological or theological interpretation, even if it comes out of black experience.

African Personality

Ezekiel Mphahlele's vision of African humanity begins with his concern for the expression of African artists' search for an

African expression. This African expression constitutes African Personality; that art inspired by an African sense of aesthetics, values and aspirations. Mphahlele's concern is for those artists who have come under the tutelage and influence of the Western artists and culture. He wants to redirect their attention to their cultural roots as source of inspiration.

Mbiti is critical of Mphahlele's position because it creates a possibility of having as many African Personalities as there are artists. He protests that the manifestation of African Personality——if such a thing exists——cannot be the preserve of the artist only. He charges that such an idea only helps to churn up a lot of emotion and does not provide a service to African people. He further argues that the meaning of "African Personality" is not clear, so no one knows what to do with it, when and if "it" actually exists. Wanting to come to terms with this elusive concept, Mbiti states,

> Whatever is or is done with it, African Personality has become one of the fields in which the African diaspora is scattered, searching for new homelands, identity, security and meaning in life. There are those who pin it down to biological roots, equating it, or Negritude, with "Black Africa". It has become a passion to imagine that "black" is a mystique, a virtue, and a quality of which one must and should be proud.[27]

Mbiti's association of the African diaspora with African Personality is significant. It implies that the independent countries of continental Africa have never needed to make an issue of African Personality. Mbiti has in mind here the rural African who composes the majority of African people. Even the urban African is for all purposes but an uprooted villager whose personality, though assailed by new forces of racism and capitalistic exploitation, is founded on the traditional cultural understanding. Therefore, he finds it hard to see to whom this term African "Personality" relates.

If Africans have no lost personality to look for, the idea of African personality can only be an importation from the African diaspora, therefore, not genuinely African. Mbiti is reluctant to make "African Personality" and blackness implicit in it determinative of African human identity, meaning, and security in the world. Rather, he would have everyone included in a more color-free universal concept. Hence, he is able to say:

> But [African Personality] is no more than a myth which does not take into consideration the fact that the majority of the African peoples are brown and not black. Africa is greater than "blackness", and not all its people and cultures can be reduced to the narrow categories of "Black Africa".[28]

Mbiti wants theological and even political discourse to transcend any racial particularity and focus only on a universal view of humanity. This does not mean that he does not care about racism, but he thinks that theologizing from an explicit or implicit racial particularity without transcending it can only lead to a stalemate, an impasse, with no progress towards racial understanding and reconciliation. Mbiti's position follows also from his insistence that Jesus has to be the theological norm and, that as such, Jesus must not be locked into a racial particularity.[29] Jesus is greater than culture even though he has to incarnate himself in culture. In the same way, Jesus is greater than blackness even if it means he must become black to redeem the black people. Mbiti sees Jesus to be more than blackness. Jesus is also, for Mbiti, the final point of identification for all humanity in view of the new humanity that he ushers in and the new extended family to which he invites all people.

Mbiti echoes the concerns of African political leaders who have realized that an understanding of ourselves, rooted in our own culture, is vital not only for responding to the changes taking place but also for the vision of future development. The only difference is that Mbiti's viewpoint is a theological view point while theirs is a political one.

> It is possible theologically to see development in terms of man co-working with God in the total process of creation. As such, development becomes a gift of God to man through fellow man. This puts enormous responsibility on man who thus exercises a form of stewardship over himself and the rest of creation.[30]

To be human, therefore, means taking responsibility for one's own historical destiny in the knowledge that this act is the will of God. The taking of responsibility for one's historical destiny is, in biblical terms, equivalent to the demand expressed most like by the apostle Paul to "work out your salvation with fear and trembling, for it is God who works in you to will and to act according to his good purpose."[31] It is possible for the Africans to take up the responsibility of development in al its aspects, according to Mbiti, because they have been (however forcibly) introduced to the

Western future dimension of time, particularly through Christianity. Their history can now begin to move forward instead of backward, and their vision focussed on the future.

Black Theology

In South Africa and the USA, the theological response to white domination and racism has appeared in the form of Black Theology. However, No similar response has occurred in independent Africa. Here, most theologians have either remained indifferent to Black Theology or, as Mbiti's case, (to the great astonishment of many people), have seen in it no direct relevance whatsoever to their own theological task. The question has often been asked: How can Mbiti in all honesty reach such a conclusion?

Mbiti has made an evaluation of Black theology both in the USA and in South Africa. Space does not allow me to make a detailed analysis of his 1974 article on Black Theology in the USA and the 1978 article on Black Theology in South Africa. I will only be concerned with those points that relate directly to our task here. It needs to be noted that while Mbiti is intensely aware of the pain and history out of which Black theology in the USA has emerged, and while he sees the indictment this theology brings against Western Christianity and its church, he still reacts strongly against the norm and method of Black Theology.[32] He finds the concept of blackness inappropriate for theological discourse. He complains,

> [Black Theology] wants to see "blackness" in everything. It speaks of Black God, Black Church, Black Liberation, Black this and Black that. While some theologians, notably James Cone, try to give

> a wider ontological meaning to "blackness," it is
> nevertheless, a color terminology arising out of the
> color consciousness of American society. ...In
> reading Black Theology one becomes sated by color
> consciousness. It is necessary to remind oneself that
> racial color is not a theological concept in
> Scripture.[33]

Mbiti sees no need of coloring God or Christ black in order to appreciate blackness as an instrument of divine manifestation. He is in agreement with Miles J. Jones that such an attempt to color God tends toward idolatry. It is tantamount to making God in the black human image and condition the very point Black Theology accuses White theology of being guilty. Mbiti disagrees with Black theologians over the essence of theology. He thinks blackness has taken on ideological proportions in Black Theology in spite of the fact that black peoples' skin pigmentation varies widely.[34] Mbiti questions not only the propriety of the term blackness but also the concern that has given that term theological validity, that is, liberation. While appreciating both the historical relevance and scriptural basis of liberation in Black Theology, Mbiti finds that the concern for liberation reduces theology to politics. Therefore he wonders what would become of Black Theology were liberation to be realized.

Pursuing this conviction that our primary identity is with Christ, he says that theology by its very nature ought to come out of "spontaneous joy in being a Christian, responding to life and ideas as one redeemed."[35] Mbiti sees in the redemption accomplished by Jesus the Christ much more than simply political and economic liberation. Redemption is primarily and basically a

spiritual reality that has implications for the political and socio-
economic spheres of human existence. According to Mbiti,
African theology fulfills this condition of non-ideology. But
because Black Theology is ideological, it is forced to reverse the
theological import of redemption because historically this theology
emerges out of the pain of oppression and not out of joy. Mbiti
appreciates the history behind Black theology's struggle but finds
that history an unacceptable reason for shifting the theological
emphasis to the particular and ideological. Mbiti is fighting to let
God be God, so that human beings are seen in the context of God
and not the other way round.

Mbiti has made his problem with Black Theology more
explicit in his article on Black theology in South Africa. In that
article he says that while black people in South Africa   need
political liberation, they do not need a theology of liberation. Mbiti
does not clarify exactly what he has in mind. But in light of other
pronouncements, one can safely conclude that the overlapping
implications of these two phenomena tend to make them equivalent
and Mbiti does not want to accept that, either for theology or for
the authentic liberation of a people. While the political liberation
of any people is Mbiti's concern as a human being and theologian,
one can sense that he believes that ultimate liberation can only
come through Jesus who said, "If you continue in my word, you
are truly my disciples; and you will know the truth, and the truth
will make you free."[36] While political and economic liberation
are necessary for authentic humanity, they do not exhaust the
meaning of God's redemption. One aspect of that redemption is a
personal relation to Jesus Christ. This is not always emphasized in
the radical forms of Black theology.

In his evaluation of South African Black theology, Mbiti does not raise the issue of blackness.[37] Actually, a marked shift has appeared in his views. He is more amenable to Black Theology as an aspect of African theology, while in the 1972 article, he did not see African theology and Black Theology (in the USA) as having any relevance to each other apart from a mutual academic interest. However, one still wonders whether the acceptance rests on geographical identity or on the basic theological stance of Black Theology. He highlights the issue of racism in a way that he did not do in his discussion of Black theology in the USA. There he was more irritated by the victims' insistence on blackness as the point of their pain and therefore of their theological concern. He writes,

> The South African Theology of liberation as it is presented in this book [*Black Theology: The South African Voice*] succeeds in stirring up christian conscience to take more seriously the fight against racism and its evils. Few would read the book without being aroused to feel the agonies of those who are denied their human rights in South Africa.[38]

Nonetheless, Mbiti remains critical of the South African Black theology on a number of points. He is uncomfortable with the exclusiveness implied in the color terminology, returning frequently to the implication of this theology for what he refers to as the "good white," represented by those who have suffered fighting the racist system. Lacking an analysis for differentiating structural racism from good individuals who also benefit from the former, Mbiti makes the plea that the "good whites" need to be acknowledged and included. He argues against Black Theology's presupposed alignment of black people over against White people and its implication that every white person is a racist and therefore bad or evil. He reiterates his objection by suggesting that an individualistic rather than collective view should be used in making judgments on white people in a situation of racism:

> Perhaps seen in general terms this [meaning collective labelling] is valid, and the whole apartheid ideology has institutionalized this separation. But in detail it cannot be said that every white person and missionary in South Africa is an oppressor and destroyer of African values and dignity. Credit should be given where it is due.[39]

Mbiti's strong reaction to some of what he considers excesses in Black Theology rests on his particular understanding of what theology is or should be. For him, God-talk has to maintains its transcendental viewpoint in order to avoid equating it with political theologies, which he sees as immanentist and, as we have already noted, theologies on their heads. Political and economic liberation does not exhaust the redemption of God even though it is part of God's ongoing work. It follows then that theology must maintain a universal viewpoint. This means that there is need for a universal and inclusive norm and that norm is Jesus. It is only in terms of this norm, without any color restrictions, that Christian anthropology can be done and properly understood. Mbiti adopts a traditional academic view of theology, which has often lacked historical engagement in the understanding of its tasks. This is why he is able to say that the black people in South Africa need political liberation, but not a theology of liberation. He betrays a view of theology that does not have a political message.

Mbiti does not see theology as primarily arising out of an existential contradiction even though his method implies such a contradiction, nor does he use a hermeneutic of suspicion to deal with the historical structures of oppression and control. Rather, he sees theology as the outcome of the encounter with Jesus. While Mbiti acknowledges history as a significant source in doing theology, he does not want historical particularity to have the final word. Rather, he subjects history to a universal norm through which he seeks to transcend race, culture, history, and theology itself. That norm is Jesus the Christ. He wants to keep Jesus Christ above color. Even though Christ is involved in the liberation of the oppressed and becomes one of the oppressed himself, yet, in a sense, he does not remain perpetually one of the oppressed Africans but becomes their liberator. As redeemer, Jesus reaches out to both the oppressed Africans and the oppressing whites; that is what makes him the liberator indeed.[40]

Mbiti sees very little benefit for black people in attempting to redefine themselves culturally and theologically from the point of their blackness. For him, culture cannot be defined into existence nor can oppression be theologized away. Only Jesus provides the true and ultimate identity and liberation, which is applicable universally. This means that theology, as reflection on the Gospel message, has much to say against racism, tribalism, oppression, and all injustices.

Jesus, Change, and African Humanity

In an article, "A Change of the African Concept of Man Through Christian Influence,"[41] Mbiti identifies some of the teaching that has affected the African view of humanity.

> In the process of evangelizing African peoples,
> missionaries have put much emphasis on the
> following elements: "the fall of man," human
> sinfulness, the need for salvation through the death
> of Jesus Christ, the Church, the Sacraments, the
> new man in Christ, the end of the world, the
> judgment and either heaven or hell. Of course there
> are other details, but this is basic structure of
> Christian teaching as it has come to us through the
> missionaries.[42]

In the idea and reality of new humanity in Jesus, which
Christianity has propagated, Mbiti finds "a very positive
contribution to the understanding of man." He asserts that this
Jesus as the human bearer of this new human image strikes a
kinship and existential note to which Africans resonate. Mbiti
observes,

> They identify themselves with Him in his various
> titles, including: Saviour, liberator, friend, helper,
> healer, protector from evil, giver of life, and
> mediator between man and God. In the African
> situation, Jesus is saviour from spirit powers,
> witchcraft and magic, misfortunes, sin and death.
> Jesus is regarded as liberator from oppression and
> colonial rule, from poverty and fear, and from all
> the forces that keep man from becoming what God
> intended him to become.[43]

The reality of Jesus brings with it the possibility of restored
wholeness, that is, in health, dignity, and excellent, wholesome
character based on a positive relationality which, in biblical terms

is equivalent to righteousness. Participation in Jesus by faith, baptism and the eucharist leads to the deification of humanity. Is this the lost golden age of Zamani? Mbiti does not say. Such a suggest would fit into his Christocentric interpretative scheme.

While the African sense of community was limited to ethnic and racial boundaries, fellowship in Christ fulfills and supersedes those identities. We do not cease to be who we are ethnically and racially, but our identity with Jesus becomes primary. We are Christians who happen to be Africans and not Africans who happen to be Christians. The theological problem with racism, tribalism, regionalism is not only that they disregard the Creator as the primary and ultimate point of reference, but they also attempt to subject God to human identities, which are given, in turn, a measure of ultimacy. Therefore, it is sinful to invest them with ultimacy and to have God subsumed under them.

In Jesus, the church becomes the new extended family that links Africans with the rest of humanity. It is a new kinship relationship that now obtains in and through the blood of Jesus Christ. This is why Mbiti condemns the divisions and racism in and outside the church as sinful.

In fellowship with Jesus, African people do not wait for death in order to enjoy a closer relation and fellowship with God, a relationship that they had no hope of ever entering. The Holy Spirit establishes them in this relationship and fellowship and through the sacraments, sustains them in it. In relationship to the new being, their humanity receives new value as it is transformed into the image and likeness of Christ, the authentic human being. It can be said that this redemption accomplished through Christ fulfills the humanizing process by which African peoples have constantly attempted to fulfill themselves, even as they progressed from one rite of passage to the next. It is also the means by which all dilemmas and quests that push African humanity to the edge of despair are resolved.

Jesus and the African View of Time

Mbiti has identified three forces that have combined to produce a change in Africans' conception of time: Christianity, Western education, and modern technology.[44] Public manifestation of this change are the adoption of national planning for economic growth and political and educational developments. Of the three forces, none has affected the African conception of time more profoundly than Christianity. It has forced Africans' orientation from being fixation on the Zamani to focusing on a Christ-centered eschatology.

Jesus is the one who reversed the flow of time by virtue of who he is and what he did. Three elements are crucial for Mbiti in speaking Christologically: the historical fact of incarnation, the cross, and the resurrection. Each is crucial in the reversal of the perception of time; without them humanity has nothing to hope for. The resurrection means escaping from the fate of being lost in the Zamani, bringing humanity permanently into the dimension of the present, and restoring to humanity what the Zamani had taken. The resurrection also introduces a future expectation:

> It is only the resurrection of those in Christ which protects them from the subtracting effects of the *Tene* (past) period which...drags the individual towards oblivion and obliteration, and robs him of his being. Now the resurrection puts a halt to this

process and reverses the whole momentum of Time.[45]

This reversal leads from death, corruptibility, change, and hopelessness to fullness of life in Christ. For Mbiti, the Christ-Event itself changes all human understanding of time. He regrets that much spiritual and doctrinal damage has already been done by accommodating Jesus' sense of time to the Western linear mode. Jesus introduces to our sense of time an eternal dimension, it is with that dimension in mind that Jesus speaks of times and seasons. As a result of this eternal dimension, emphasis on human destiny shifts from the future or past, as the case may be, to the present, understood as an ontological present and not a temporal present. In relating time to the hope of a new creation, Mbiti observes, "Only when the past and future dimensions of Time are summed up into one dimension, in the presence of God, would the new creation really become evident, for that is truly the end of Time, not by its elimination but by its consummation."[46] The fact of the resurrection places Jesus in what Mbiti calls a "dimensionless present, the presence of God" until all things are summed up in Jesus and subjected to God's presence. For Mbiti, that sort of consummation is the true teleological End. The present reality of this unfolding eschatological vision gives to Christianity the "terrible responsibility of pointing the way to that ultimate Identity, Foundation and Source of security."[47]

European intrusion and the colonial interlude were disastrous for black humanity. Mission theology in collusion with colonialism brought a Gospel that had been in many ways compromised and subjected to racial and cultural hegemony and an imperialistic rule whose primary motivation was the capitalistic self-interest of the ruling race. In order to reclaim their own selfhood, the African people have resisted all hegemonic forces and sought political, cultural, socio-economic, and theological independence. While achievement of all the above-named is necessary and wonderful, the most fundamental and ultimate change or revolution that African humanity needs, according to Mbiti, is the new humanity through faith in Jesus, by which they find their selfhood and become truly self-determining. It is this identity with Christ that makes economic, social, and political changes ultimately meaningful and humanizing.

CHAPTER SIX

BEING HUMAN IN AFRICA:
Dilemma of Appropriate definition

It is just over two decades ago now since Mbiti offered to the public his interpretation of African philosophy and religion. A number of his ideas have received a fair amount of criticism of varying intensity.[1] But no one yet has either tried to offer as comprehensive a religious and philosophical interpretation of African culture as Mbiti has done nor given a comprehensive critique of his overall interpretation. The criticisms have failed to dislodge the thrust of his theoretical and phenomenological framework. The task that I set for myself was not to overthrow Mbiti's interpretative paradigm but rather to rearrange it in order to strengthen it at points I consider weak. I do this in the conviction that Mbiti's thinking, with some corrections, would serve as a much more solid basis for African human identity and thereby contribute much more positively to the construction of an African Christian anthropology.

I believe Mbiti is right in maintaining that African ontology is the most suitable point of departure for understanding African religion and philosophy. Since he is writing as a Christian theologian, he is also right in asserting that the Gospel functions to fulfil African culture in so far as African culture is also the *preparatio evangelica*. However, Mbiti errs by making time, and particularly his conception of African time, the hermeneutic key for African ontology. In doing so, he neglects the true hermeneutic key: ontological relationality, which he actually acknowledges to be the basis of the African world view as it is clearly implied in his dictum: "I am because we are, and since we are, therefore I am."

Debate on the Concept of Time

No part of Mbiti's writing has provoked more criticism, commentary, and heated debate than his views on the African concept of time, in particular, his denial of a future dimension. Kwesi Dickson tells of a heated debate that followed one of Mbiti's presentation on the concept of time. While many African scholars took exception to various aspects of Mbiti's view, Dickson reports: "It is with regard to the future that the keenest debate was generated by Mbiti's exposition, and the general opinion seemed to be that the concept of the future—and not merely a myopic future—is known."[2] Kwesi Dickson's own opinion is that Mbiti has oversimplified the African view of time.[3] He points out that the existence of the idea of judgment and retribution in some African societies supports the view that a future dimension of time does actually exist. Furthermore, Kwesi Dickson mentions that the idea of destiny, which is prevalent in Ghana, points to a future dimension of time.

Benjamin Ray shares Dickson's view that Mbiti has not taken the idea of destiny into account.[4] Ray states that in Africa, as in the West, time moves forward and, therefore, the future cannot be denied. A short future is not the same as no future at all.

Lugano Sankey says that to deny the reality of a future is to deny any hope to a people. He argues that many human activities are an investment in the future.[5] Sankey is right on both counts; his point has serious implications for the nature of African humanity in light of Mbiti's view that African time lacks of a future dimension.

John Parratt, who generally agrees with Mbiti's emphasis on the past as the African temporal focal point, finds fault with Mbiti's assertion that Africans have no sense of future time. He thinks that the process of the rites of passage implies passage of time and, therefore, anticipation of the future. While Mbiti touches on this process, for him it does not imply a sense of the future point, but only a movement of time into the past.[6]

Mbiti contradicts himself when he says that future time can only be reckoned as potential time because it contains no events to transform it into actual time. Because he denies a future dimension of time, partly due to his own definition, he cannot then start talking about potential time. Potential time may not indeed be actual time, but it is conceived as time all the same. To call it potential does not stop its actualization. The only difference is that actual time has a historical imprint while potential time is a mental anticipation. By qualifying his definition of time and dividing it into actual and potential time, Mbiti makes a case against himself.

Francis Gillies thinks that the rhythm of nature, which Mbiti acknowledges as a confirmation of cyclic time only, actually affirms future time. He states:

> Now, this category "future", discernible in Bantu time is essentially the same as the concept of an "infinite future" in western time. The concept of the infinite time in western countries is founded upon chronological time, not, as Mbiti argues on ontologically linear time. It is a fundamental biological category, dictated by hunger. It is a

universal category in man.[7]

Gilles's charge is tantamount to saying that Mbiti has not only misunderstood the nature of linear time but has also made it normative in his understanding of African time, thereby misunderstanding both.

Mbiti's insistence that Zamani is the controlling dimension of African view of time has also been criticized. Benjamin Ray thinks that Mbiti fails to recognize the important dimension of ritual time. Ray asserts that ritual time is cyclic. It interrupts ordinary linear time and recovers the mythical past. He explains: "In ritual time, the mythical past is far from being a 'graveyard'. On the contrary, it is a constant source of ontological renewal through the ritual re-enactment of primordial acts."[8] In other words, the past is not only important for itself, as Mbiti would have us believe, but also because of its significant meaning for the present. The present and the past stand in a dialectical relationship. The conception of time is not a one-way street. Therefore, Ray points out that to speak of the past as irrecoverable is a total misrepresentation. It seems to Ray that Mbiti has simplified not only the future dimension but also the past, both in the way the past is reckoned and how it is related to the present.

E.A. Ruch, who is very sympathetic to Mbiti's view, also alludes to the ritual linkage between the past and the present:

> . . . . legends and similar mythical narratives...not
> children's tales, told for amusement, ...share in the
> central reality of myth. Their aim is to keep alive
> the root and origin of the tribe, the continuously
> renewed source of its life. The evocation of the

myth of origin is part of the sacred ritual, which has as its function not merely to narrate, but through the mythical effectiveness of the word, to make present this origin with all its primeval abundance of cosmogonic power. As was indicated above, the *eschaton* of the Africans lies in the past, not in a sense of an original paradise of which one can have little more than fond memories or legendary reports, but in the sense of an entity which can always be "re-presented" ritually, yet very effectively.[9]

While generally agreeing with Mbiti on the backward movement of time and focus of attention, unlike Mbiti, Ruch does not want to fossilize the past but rather to make it accessible to the present as a living and not a dead end.

Following Mircea Eliade's view that to "ancient man" time implied the cycle of primeval acts, John Parratt asserts that the ritual year becomes crucial in the way traditional societies conceived time.[10] Parratt argues in support of Mbiti that such cyclic time is grounded in the past, and that the ritual year attempts to recreate within the present time the benefits of a mythical or bygone time. However, John Parratt differs from Ruch's position by focusing on the benefits of the past rather than the ontological relationship.

Ray raises another feature of an African view of time. He says that there is not just one time, but a variety of times: mythical time, historical time, ritual time, agricultural time, seasonal time, solar time, lunar time. Each of these times has its own duration and quality.[11] This way of looking at time may easily follow from the very definition of time that Mbiti advances. However, Ray is positing a plurality of times, not a singularity of time, as Mbiti's definition implies. If events define time, why should there not be as many kinds of times as there are recurring events? Ray's view is closer to Kwesi Dickson's argument that Mbiti has oversimplified his view of African time. However, there are within African societies certain dominant modes of reckoning time.

In Blake Wiley Burleson, Mbiti has an advocate who, in my opinion, instead of doing Mbiti's view justice, introduces more confusion. In his doctoral dissertation, "John Mbiti: The Dialogue of an African Theologian with African Traditional Religion", Burleson understands the concept of time from the point of view of the History of Religion School. He thinks that most criticism directed at Mbiti by theologians and anthropologists "is misdirected and misses the essence of Mbiti's thought."[12] He argues that Mbiti has never said that traditional Africans do not have a capacity to conceive of a future, but rather that there is "virtually no future." Burleson thinks Mbiti is saying that the "vision of the distant future has no place in traditional life."[13] I think Burleson interprets Mbiti's denial of an infinite future accurately. He also agrees with Mbiti that traditional Africans do not conceive of time as a linear forward movement of events and that this being the case, there can be no future dimension of time. It is just this interpretation that I find problematic in Mbiti and Burleson. Their denial of a significant future dimension raises the question of the standard which is used in the understanding of time against which the traditional African concept is judged. It is clear to me that the two have as a standard the Western linear model of time in determining the length of the future. It is actually the African view that has an infinite future dimension because the

African view is not teleological in the Christian and Western sense of the word. It cannot be quantified and has no *eschaton*.

For Burleson, the African conception of time is cyclic. He criticizes Mbiti for overstating the argument against a future dimension for the sake of emphasis. Burleson finds the key to understanding Mbiti in identifying Mbiti's Sasa with what Eliade calls Profane Time [14] and Zamani with the archetypal myth of Eternal Return.[15] Burleson seems to make this identification because Mbiti conceives Zamani as the dead end of all history. As it has been pointed out, this interpretative model by Eliade is not a true representation of the Zamani and, therefore, not helpful in clarifying an African view of time. Africans conceive Zamani ontologically; it is time full of events done by their ancestors. It is linked to the Sasa, which is the time of ontological intensity. The Sasa becomes a time of being human and therefore of making and remembering history. Zamani is not simply the archetypal mythical time; it is telescoped historical ontology. Burleson, like Mbiti and many anthropologists, uncritically assume that traditional Africans have a simple cyclical view of time.[16] Ruch is closer to the truth:

> African man, on the other hand, does not fully stretch out the cyclical time of the myth. Like a helicoidal spring, his time retains the loops of the nature's eternal return, while at the same time acquiring a linear progression from the past to the future. The comparison with the helicoidal spring has another application: African time is more elastic than western time. The precise dating of events and even their chronological sequence are less important than the events themselves and the lessons they offer. ...The cyclic return is mixed with the linear progress.[17]

The point is that an African view of time must be based not simply on western models from hellenist and modern times but on factors and perceptions that constitute time in African society itself. Some of those factors and perceptions will be discussed below as we subject Mbiti's concept of time to more critical examination and correction.

A Critique of Mbiti's Position

It is clear from our survey of criticism of Mbiti's understanding of time as key to African ontology that it has some serious problems to be generally accepted by most Africanist scholars. When applied specifically to African understanding of humanity, I think it has serious limitations. Let us look at some of those limitations.

The concept of time is not the key to African ontology. The reasons for this assertion will become clear as I discuss what I consider to be the most serious flaws in his concept of time in their appropriate place below.

Humanity is Over Time

By making it key, the concept of time has some false implications for African humanity. In Mbiti's concept of time, humanity is made subject to time and captive to a mythical past, leaving virtually no room for the creative imagination of the African people.

While Mbiti rightly acknowledges the anthropocentric nature of the African world view, he thinks that the concept of time presents a better key to understanding African ways. By making time normative, he sacrifices human agency and its use of time. The concept of time is important in historiography and in eschatology, but in anthropology, other factors make time comparatively relative in the determination of human character. By emphasizing the past as the most dominant aspect of time and by denying a future dimension, Mbiti actually makes African peoples captive to the past dimension of time.[18] By so doing, he unwittingly portrays them as lacking the imagination to be agents of their own history. They become children of nature who are simply shaped by nature. Thus it seems logical to Mbiti to say,

> So African people have no "belief in progress", the idea that development of human activities and achievements move from a low to a higher degree. The people neither plan for the distant future nor "build castles in the air." The center of human thought and activities is the Zamani period, towards which Sasa moves.[19]

If the African peoples indeed have no sense of development or progress or improvement, what Mbiti says may be acceptable. However, African history and prehistory tell us a very different story. On the continent of Africa, progress was made in many sphere of human development, and much of it native to Africa. Not all African peoples progressed culturally and technologically in the same ways and at the same time. It is actually these differences in progress that in part encouraged trade between distant peoples. The new connotations that the word progress has taken since the Seventeenth century as a result of the Industrial Revolution in Europe, should not invalidate the view that much progress did not occur in previous times on other continents. To use progress in relation to Africa is not to impose a term that is not applicable to the African situation because nothing of comparable technological magnitude took place, but rather recognition of the essential historical meaning of the phenomenon signified in the term.[20] The rapidity of modern western progress is not the norm for human progress, but one aspect of it. Because the progress of the ancients in Africa was of a different scale and at a different pace does not mean that they did not plan for the future, as Mbiti has asserted.

Africans have been active participants in the making of their own history and have utilized time by responding to it appropriately. As makers of their own history, they view the past as significant for the present and to guide them into the future. The past is not important only for itself, as Mbiti seems to insist, but also because it is ontologically and existentially linked to the present and especially to the future. In other words, the three dimensions of time imply one another.

Reality of a Future Dimension

By denying the presence of the future, Mbiti makes the Zamani overblown and human vision oriented to the past and not to the future. The African conception of time does have a future dimension of time. The Africans plan for the future and invite their living-dead to move into it with them. Africans indeed have looked to the past for wisdom in order to survive in the present and the anticipated future. But it seems to me that Mbiti denies the future in order to legitimize acceptance of Christian eschatology which, for him, introduces the future dimension. More seriously, for him the Christian eschatology actually becomes the yardstick for understanding the nature of African time.

Mbiti is wrong in asserting that African time has virtually no future and confers on the past a quality of frigidity or deadness it does not possess. The Africans bring the past along with them and celebrate it as ontological ritual time. The absence of written history based on a numerical calendar led Africans to place more emphasis on human relationships and ritual and to view history sacrally. Therefore, it does not follow, as Mbiti would have us believe, that the future is silent and meaningless beyond the reckoning of a year or two. Rather, the experience of the past raises expectations for the future. Mbiti speaks of people's expectations but denies them the expected future time and events. Realistically speaking, "Endlessness or Eternity," even on Mbiti's terms, is not in the past. Rather, the past, the present, and the future together constitute that Endlessness. Endlessness or Eternity is the sum of all dimensions of time as existentially experienced and anticipated.

The question of the movement of time is a subtle and illusive one. For Mbiti to speak of the movement of time and then to deny a future dimension is a contradiction in terms. It denies a people a consciousness of time. The very fact of a past dimension implies a future dimension. Each implies the other in our consciousness of them. What moves into the past did not exist at one time because it belonged to a future time.

If natural phenomena are the events that mark time, then they either have their origin in the future because they are always expected to come from the future or they grow out of the past or arise spontaneously with the present. The next rain, harvest, child, initiation, and even death are all perceived to "occur" in the future as anticipated events. From the future, they move through the present where they are actualized on their way into the past, which is their historical destiny. The present is the meeting point of the past and the future. At this point of encounter, the future is actualized and the past advanced forward in one and the same event. However, it is legitimate to speak also of both an advancing past and future or a receding past and future, because we experience the movement of time both ways.

Other phenomena grow out of the past into the present with possibility for future developments. Food is sown as an investment for future use. Fruit trees are a more long-term investment. The present serves as the past's region of elongation, to use a biological metaphor. Our own sense of growth and development and our sense of ourselves as perceiving subjects further help us to view time as three-dimensional instead of two-dimensional. Time and events move at one crucial point in two opposite directions: the future swelling the past and the past progressing towards the future. In this way we can speak of both a Zamani and a Future from our present actuality. It is more realistic to speak of a three-dimensional and two-directional instead of a two-dimensional and one-directional movement of time. We experience time as moving in two directions, past and future, whether we reckon time linearly or not. Only in this way can one avoid the paradoxes that Mbiti resorts to when explaining death, judgment and destiny as future events.

Our own existence is one of those events that mark out time. This existence is crucial and critical because it demands a determination of what constitutes a meaningful and significant time or event, thereby giving meaning to time and history. Mbiti's insight that African people make time is important if he means that human agency is crucial to the understanding of time. However, I doubt if Mbiti means it in this way, even though it is capable of this interpretation. The crucial role of human agency in humanizing time, so to speak, adds weight to my first point above which denies the subjection of humanity to time.

The ancestors are both in the past and in the future. Historically, they lived in the past and died in the past, but existentially, they are a present and future reality. We live in the hope of joining them in the Future. Since death has transformed their mode of existence, they are, in one sense, gone ahead of us and we can look forward to joining them. They transcend temporal time and continue to live in the present. Such a view assumes some distinctions between historical and spiritual living. The living participate more intensely in the historical aspect while the living-dead participate more intensely in spiritual aspect of human existence. Being out of the historical realm of living, the ancestors are not fixed in the past but are present with the living. It seems to me that it is a mistake to impose historical time on the existence of those in the spiritual realm.

In light of the above discussion,[21] Mbiti's definition of time is inadequate. By restricting it simply to events without taking into account the human agency in determining the meaning of time, he takes too narrow a view. The significance of time in Africa is that time is fundamentally ontological because we are conscious of it regardless of events. Time is not simply phenomenological. The very fact of our being alive, in Mbiti's terms, is the one event that determines the meaning of time.

Time is conceived objectively as a reality in its own right by African peoples. Therefore, Mbiti's category of No-Time is meaningless. The fact that time is reckoned in relation to events, whether of natural or human agency, does not rob time of its separate existence. There is a sense in which time is a given and not a human creation. History, which is the human meaning of time, is indeed a human creation, but time per se is not. Mbiti's definition of African time, which associates it only with events, confuses history and time. However, there is a dynamic relationship between time, events, and the human actor and interpreter. This relationship gives rise to historical consciousness. All three are dynamically synchronized, and the result is that both history and time apparently move forward and backward. People in Africa are conscious of the passage of time even when nothing significant is happening. Time is not static and neither are the people; they speak of time being gone and of losing time.[22] Africans can conceive of the future, not simply as potential time but, for the collective group, as assured time also, because ontologically they are moving toward it even as it seems to be moving toward them. Mbiti maintains that time as a separate reality does not move and that only events come and go.[23] Lugano Sankey agrees with him, at least for once, on this point. But my view is that Africans are conscious of a double movement involving time and events relative to human existence. If everything else came to a standstill, we would still be conscious of the passage of time relative to the stillness of things, because we are conscious beings and the major event in creation that determines the meaning of time.

Even though Sasa includes aspects of the future as Mbiti concedes, it does not exhaust the future. The future exists as the anticipated actual dimension of time. This is why people plan for the future. Parents look forward to having grandchildren, to getting old, or saving for the future. Someone in Africa who says, "these days," indeed has in mind a short past, a present, and a short future, but the short future implicit in "these days" does not exhaust the future dimension of time. Africans are conscious of both an indefiniteness and an infinity of time. These may not be conceived in numerical terms but arise out of their own sense of being and experience. If time is two-directional, it is a contradiction to say that Zamani, which is a dimension of time, is also the graveyard of time.

Time and Human Character

When it comes to explaining the nature of evil, so significant an aspect in understanding humanity, Mbiti's concept of time is completely inapplicable.

Focusing more on the historical than the cosmic aspect of the African self-understanding, Mbiti points out the significance of character for maintaining personal and societal integrity. What he says about the Yoruba is applicable to almost all African societies:

> Character is the essence of Yoruba ethics, and upon it depends even the life of a person. So the people say, "Gentle character, it is which enables the rope of life to stay unbroken in one's hands", and again, "It is good character that is man's guard."[24]

Character has much to do with the human vocation and it is indispensable for the creation of what Thomas Cullen Young has called the "Good Village."[25] Engelbert Mveng tells us that the proper human vocation is to safeguard the integrity and the unity of the immense cosmic network. The moral law not only governs individual acts and relationships with the next of kin and God, but it also regulates our relationship with the world in its minute details and globalness.[26] Mveng has beautifully stated the link between personal character and the world in the following statement: "It is the divided person who divides the world."[27] Therefore, the integrity of personal character has great significance for the multi-faceted world order. To hold society responsible is to hold individuals responsible. Societal good or evil has individual creators. Mbiti is absolutely right to emphasize a dynamic ethical conception when he says that "a person is what he is because of what he does, rather than that he does what he does because of what he is." However, I beg to differ with Mbiti when he distinguishes between the morality of "being" and the morality of "conduct".[28] Conduct is an expression of being; no abstract being or state of being exists apart from the acting being and his or her acts.

Mbiti's assertion that moral being rests on doing may help to address the imbalance in the doctrine of Original Sin, which has explained the morality of conduct in terms of being. But the biblical description of the primal sin supports the opposite view: it was evil conduct that actually led to the immorality of being. This is why God holds even sinful human beings responsible and continues to expect obedience from them. The uniqueness of Jesus is that he was obedient all the way, even unto death. In other words, he maintained the integrity of his humanity. This is what makes him sinless. Africa's emphasis on morality of conduct as defining human beings morally may be its contribution to correcting unacceptable aspects of the doctrine of Original Sin such as viewing sin as a genetic inheritance.

The dilemma expressed by Paul in Romans 7:14-20, in which he expresses his failure to do the good that he wants to do, and his tendency instead to do the evil he wants to avoid, is as much an experience of African people, whether Christian or not. It is out of an existential moral contradiction between being and doing that African people become aware of their evil heart. The matter of accountability for this existential contradiction cannot be explained by Mbiti's concept of time. When time as conceived by Mbiti is applied to death, it produces an unnecessary paradox.

Death as a Future Event

Mbiti concedes that death is one event that is certain to occur at some future time, and he states that this is a paradox. Even in Africa where infant mortality rate is very high, acceptable death is associated with old age. This paradox, which is actually a contradiction, should have alerted Mbiti to a problem in his conception of time. One cannot deny a future dimension and then slip it in under the guise of a paradox. The plain fact is that death is indeed anticipated in the future because there is a future dimension to the African conception of time.

Mbiti has discovered a false paradox because he has imposed our historical time frame on the world of the Spirits. For him, the Spirits are in the Zamani instead of being a present reality, who live with their people, not only in memory,[29] but even more vitally, ontologically. Secondly, having rejected the existence of a future, Mbiti is forced to create one in order to accommodate the reality of death, an event as certain to happen in future as daybreak or nightfall. Since death is in the future, people hoping to grow to old age would not limit that future to the next two years or so. Thirdly, Mbiti does not take into account the fact that death transforms time and historical perception in such a way that our historical reckoning of time must be adjusted when we speak of the dead. As Ruch observes:

> Beyond the span of time covered by living witnesses, however, the factual content of the narrative begins to blur into legend. ...Time is frozen in a kind of unchangeable *aevum* in which nothing new ever happens and in which chronological sequence of events are no longer meaningful. This does not mean that the facts themselves, which have already moved into the Zamani, are considered less important or irrelevant. *On the contrary, the passage of time has given the legends a new value, an aura of sacredness and respectability, which prevents critical questions from even arising. The events narrated have shifted from the realm of human history to that of quasi-religious faith.* [My emphasis][30]

This shift of history to a different level of perception is an important observation that Mbiti's view of time acknowledges, but does not take into account. Even though Ruch has followed Mbiti's view of past and future rather uncritically, on this point he departs from him by giving significance to the transformation that occurs.

Mbiti's use of memory as the criterion for making the distinction between the living-dead and the spirits is not warranted. All dead people are spirits and they are all living-dead, remembered or not. It is a general belief in many societies that the spirits are always with the living. Theirs is not a static and frozen existence as Ruch would have us think. Memory and ritual attach the living not only to the "living-dead" as defined by Mbiti but to the whole spirit world.

Salvation and Time

Mbiti is convinced a two-dimensional concept of time, allows no future hope and destiny for humankind.[31] The result is that among many African peoples, Mbiti points out, their sense of salvation is very utilitarian, just as their worship is. He writes, "When individuals and communities get satisfactory amounts of food, children, rain, health and prosperity, they have approached something of the original state."[32] According to his reckoning, the golden age can only be in the past. As that original state recedes further and further from the present, it becomes more and more unattainable.

Humanity is constantly in search of lost harmony and cosmic hospitality by seeking to overcome, through ritual and sacrifice, the cosmic and personal hostilities and alienations that are constantly experienced as a threat to life itself. Since there is no scheme of salvation that can bypass death, the ultimate threat, human beings have devised rituals that prepare and help them to face death. The initiation rites that dramatize the victory of life over death, according to Engelbert Mveng,[33] are to Africans, what baptism, which represents death and the resurrection, is to Christians. The salvific value is in the incorporation of the individual into the common life of the whole community of the living and dead, and through that community, the rest of the cosmos with God. Iloanusi calls this salvational self-fulfillment. It involves the whole person and others in community. It is salvation with and for others in and with the world.[34]

Salvation in African terms, according to Iloanusi, is a move from individualism to community, from hostility to hospitality, material poverty to material prosperity, sickness to health, from vulnerability to the power of witches to protection against their power, from unfaithfulness to integrity, from death to life. Salvation is for this life because beyond death one is safe and secure forever.[35] Only the wicked get punished and these are those who worked with and for the forces of death against other people. But in Mbiti's discussion of death, he seems to forget that death introduces a new key in human existence transforming it into spiritual levels of existence. While spiritual identity for individual spirits may not be remembered by the living, the collective identity is part of the memory of those still living. The personal and collective remembrance is important in maintaining the relationship between the two. Contrary to Mbiti's assertion that death puts the living-dead on their long journey to Zamani, it is their transformation to a spiritual level of existence and the collective memory of all the departed that makes their presence possible to the living community.

Teleology or Deteriology?

Mbiti paints a very grim picture of the last phase of human existence before a human being is translated into the spirit world:

> Death is a gradual removal of the individual, as a person without the body...from the moment of intense consciousness to one of shadowy existence, from the *mituki* period of remembrance by personal

names to one of being forgotten as a spirit. For the Akamba death is only the final process of disintegration...being lost from the intensity of living to the obscurity of the *tene* horizon. It is a departure for home, but relative to human beings that "home" is one where the individual finally disappears, melts away into existence without "personal names" and hence without personality, deprived of the totality of being. ...God does not recreate what at death has begun to disintegrate. There is no teleology in African eschatology; what there is might be called "Deteriology"...[36]

Mbiti's grim picture is not shared by other writers on the subject. Bimwenyi-Kweshi holds the opposite view. He is more pessimistic about human existence in the present period of intense living, in which humanity lives like a fugitive.[37] The intense desire for life drives human beings to look forward to the victory of life over death, to a life that lasts. The everlastingness of this life is neither dependent upon remembrance nor on "personal immortality" through procreation, as Mbiti maintains, but only on the overcoming of death. This view is shared by Mveng.[38] Iloanusi says that the highest goal of human existence is the achievement of immortality by joining the ancestral world.[39] I think that these writers present a far fuller picture of what many African peoples—— at least those from the part of Africa I am familiar with——believe and hope than Mbiti does. It seems to me that Mbiti overplays the dimness of future prospects in African religious traditions in order to create room for the great prospect that Christianity offers. He seems to see, not continuity between African and Christian eschatologies, but a radical discontinuity, in spite of his claim that traditional culture and religiosity are the *preparatio evangelica* and are fulfilled by the Gospel. His poetry too manifests the same lack of hope.[40]

Mbiti is correct in maintaining that an eschatology does not exist within the African religious tradition, but he is not right in saying that instead of a teleology there is a deteriology. He says that as long as children are born and generation succeeds generation, there can be no end to the world. However, the continuation of the world does not abrogate the reality of a human personal end. It is a personal end conceived as the transformation of the physical or historical existence into a spiritual existence by way of death while human history goes on. As I have argued before, this memory is not the factor that keeps humanity on the living-dead. To become spirit is to cease being historically human but not the deterioration of humanity. It is the upgrading of humanity from historical to spiritual existence through death. Even though death affects existence in some very radical ways, it does not have the last word on life itself. Though death is a tragic human reality of cosmic proportions, it is at the same time, as Bimwenye-Kweshi described it, the gateway to life that lasts. The deep ontological desire is to live long and well in this life as a preparation for the next. Mbiti is right in maintaining that Africans do not think of history as such coming to an end, but individual histories do come to an end. Finally, everyone ends up as spirit. African religious thought does possess a teleology, but it is more a teleology of personal historical existence rather than a teleology of history and the world as is the case in Christian eschatology.

Particularity and Universality

In addition to criticisms of Mbiti's African concept of time, critics have also focused on his rejection of Blackness, Negritude and African Personality as concepts of any use in African peoples' self-understanding and self-definition. The reconception and commodification of time brought about during the colonial interlude was not as fundamental a change in the experience of the African people as Mbiti maintains. Rather, it is the bitter experiences of racism and domination that had the most traumatic effect on their sense of being.[41] Mbiti does not see any virtue in drawing attention to the fact of one's blackness. He thinks that those who use such concepts as negritude and African personality mystify what should not. He has questioned the value of coining these new terminologies, and has wondered whether these terms have any valid meaning, especially for the rural masses. Mbiti is not blind to racism but he fails to grant it the theological significance that it deserves and the seriousness with which it must be challenged on every front.

It is not a matter of mystique, virtue, or quality, in calling attention to one's skin color as black people. If nothing hideous had happened as a result of skin color, it would be unnecessary to dramatize its significance and beauty. However, it is the negative response that blackness has evoked from white people which makes it necessary to put the record straight by those who know what it means to be black humanity. The realization that such a negative response is not deserved, has automatically led to self-affirmation. Only black people have been subjected to such oppressive and humiliating treatment on account of their skin pigmentation by those who have claimed superiority of race. It makes all the difference in the world to one's sense of being whether one is defined by others, and negatively at that, or by oneself. Since experience has shown that black humanity is viewed negatively, it is only the black people who can show pride in it and struggle for its positive image, otherwise, the forces unleashed by hatred of black humanity, which are usually associated with black-phobia, will tread that image into the dust of racism. To stand guard against threats to one's being is not an obsession. Therefore, Mbiti's rejection of the emphasis on blackness as a personal, cultural, and theological matter, in turn needs to be rejected as based on existential and historical amnesia.[42]

Colonial Kenya provides a significant case of racism and domination reigning supreme. How can Mbiti, as a Kenyan, overlook this case? He also fails to appreciate the pervasiveness of racism in a world where some races dominate and set themselves and their technological-know-how as norms for defining and dominating others. Judged by the attitudes of many white people, missionaries included, it seems that Africans collectively have been damned by nature to a subservient role among all human beings. They were destined to be the servants of all. This view of the dominant race is reflected in a statement by Dr. Alexander Hetherwick, a Scottish missionary to Malawi.

> Remembering, then, all the past history of the African race and of all it has suffered and come through at the hands of the older, abler and more powerful races in the human family, one has many a time asked oneself what has Africa got to bring? ...and I can see the African bringing into the fold his gift of patience and that brave unmurmuring endurance of injustice and wrong which have enabled him to hold up his head amid all the horrors and cruelties of slavery and the slave traffic. ...And when I remember that patience and

uncomplaining endurance of wrong were seen at
their highest on the cross, I can almost hear the
voice of the Lord standing by the treasury of the
Church of God and saying, as he notes the African
approaching with his contribution to the temple,
"This man has cast in more than they all." [43]

This is the kind of talk that makes a mockery of God and the
Gospel. Furthermore, it makes the missionary movement suspect.
Hetherwick's very spiritualization of injustice and cruelty against
the African people, the way he offers them as global examples of
sacrificial suffering, shows the odds against which the African
people had to run up against both in living under this cultural-
religious colonialism and in resisting it. It is against these
spiritualized cultural and ideological underpinnings of colonialism
that Leopold Sedar Senghor and Ezekiel Mphahlele were struggling
in seeking to redefine the African.

Therefore, to assert one's ethnic identity as an exercise in
self-definition with a view to self-liberation and self-determination
is not to become a racist in return. Mbiti does not need to be
reminded that African nationalism was partly a struggle against the
negative view of, ill-treatment of, and racism against black
people. Nationalism carried out a black agenda. The struggle was
not simply against an unrepresentative system of government but
against a Christianity, a government and a colonial system that was

and dignity. Africa needs to redefine itself theoretically as well as pragmatically. In this process, Africa must draw up a humanizing agenda in all aspects of its life in order to stop the humiliation and domination of many centuries and to avoid natural and human forces from wreaking havoc on future generations.

Although African theology missed its historically opportune moment to engage in the redefinition of black humanity at the time of nationalistic struggle for freedom and independence, the need for redefinition still exist. The issue is more urgent today than ever before because it is more than thirty years overdue. South African blacks and Africa-Americans should not be left to wrestle with the issue alone. As long as white racism against black people is a fact of life anywhere in the world, indeed even regardless of that racism, blackness remains the fact and symbol of our ontological and cultural identity, and racial solidarity, whether we like it or not. And as long as development, which is the major socio-political and cultural preoccupation of the African countries, continues to lag behind, our blackness is being made by racists into our badge of shame and not of honor.[45] Integrity of character and responsibility are a must for development that is humane. Being ontologically significant, blackness cannot but be theologically imperative for African theology and for socio-cultural and politico-economic issues. The concept of time cannot deal with all these matters because it simply does not apply to them.

On Mbiti's assertion that Negritude is elitist, the same criticism can be made on theology. How many rural people are engaged in systematic theology? Of course, Mbiti knows that oral theology takes place in the villages, but can he be so sure that there is no conscious pride of being culturally African and black in the villages? Villagers may not call this pride Negritude, just as they do not call their reflection of faith Oral theology, but each is a reality. The very fear that "tribalism" is an obstacle to the process of democratization indicates peoples' deeply ingrained pride in their identity. That pride will need to be harnessed to some more inclusive vision. The majority of the Mau-Mau fighters against white settlement in Mbiti's native Kenya were not elites, yet one factor in addition to the land issue that motivated them was their cultural pride as Kikuyu.

Or take Mbiti's contention that Negritude is a myth. Senghor does not deny that Negritude is a myth, but myths have epistemological and existential value. In a world of change and new experiences there is always room for new myths, these may be ideological, pseudo-scientific, or folk myths, but all function in the same way. In a sense, African nationalism was one massive expression of Negritude, and the participation of the rural masses was crucial to its manifestation and eventual triumph. Negritude has contributed positively to raising black cultural consciousness to an intellectual level in a world in which only white culture and its intellectual, ideological elitism mattered.

Mbiti, as we said in the introduction and Chapter Four rejects the use of terms that are not derived from Scripture. He maintains that words such as Negritude and African Personality have no valid meaning. But Mbiti well knows that many theological concepts- Trinity, person, substance, etc.- are not found in Scripture yet have been preeminent in western theological tradition. Such terms had to be coined to describe new understandings of God. Similarly, in a racist situation skin color is an existential dilemma and deserves new terms when seeking new understanding and ways to overcome oppression. Mbiti's resistance to presenting a theology in a foreign cultural dress as relevant to African people while their authentic culture is deemed unfit for theological discourse is no different from the theological resistance that black people in the USA and South Africa offer to a situation in which white skin color is made the dominating standard. Theologians in the West have tended to relegate the race issue to the realm of social or ethical problems and not to deal with it as a theological one, while in independent Africa, race is either an embarrassment or simply dismissed as unimportant or irrelevant by both theologians and politicians. The questions that Black theology raises——how to speak of the image of God in a racist world and the theological status of blackness,——are theologically legitimate ones, if we are to get to the bottom of the racial and cultural dilemmas.

I remember how I felt when I visited South Africa in 1970. Coming from an independent African country, I had a rude awakening when suddenly my freedom was gone as I was forced to fit into prearranged racist structures. I could not define or determine myself; I had already been defined. I could not freely go into any shop or restaurant as I wanted. My choices were determined and greatly reduced. It was my humanity that was being slighted by the racist apartheid system on account of my color. The immediate gut reaction was the question, Why, God? This is a fundamentally theological question. Independence in some of our African countries need not blind us to the racism that black people face in a white-dominated world.

One of Mbiti's reasons for rejecting blackness as a theological concept is his concern for universality. Mbiti has claimed that we are first Christians and only secondly are we Africans. He has also stated that the only identity that one can claim is an identity with Christ; against that, other claims pale in significance. But can we truly dispense with our particularity for the sake of Christ and human universality? What color is Christ's identity, if Christ is not made incarnate in the color of the believer? Can a colorless Christ be at once our particularity and our universality? These are important questions that Mbiti does not address.

Jesus gives our racial particularity the stamp of his ownership by loving us unto redemption because he has come to do away with racism of every kind and to put us on the road to authentic humanity. If in Christ there is no longer Jew or Greek, no male and female, no civilized or barbarian,[46] then it follows that there is no black or white. What does this mean historically and existentially?

Jesus meets us in our historical particularity and affirms us in it so as to make it part of a history of redemption and liberation. With Jesus as redeemer, the historical struggle proves to be the establishment of the reign of God and its values against the forces of exclusion, domination, oppression, exploitation, and alienation brought about by personal and structural sin. His historical mission of bringing abundant life [47] becomes our historical project under God, the initiator of history. We saw in the second chapter that history has primarily to do with the flow and ebb of human relationships, not human exploits for their own sake.

To use the concept blackness in drawing attention to a particular existential situation or ontological dilemma does not make blackness ultimate, and need not be made ultimate. But rather, under the Gospel of Jesus, it becomes important to affirm black humanity because the legitimacy of black humanity is affirmed by the Gospel.[48]

One does not need to throw away one's particularity in order to attain to some higher universal reality of being human. Rather, one strives to realize full human integrity in one's particularity. Only in this way that one can be a responsible participant in the universal expression of humanity. We do not need to enter into the Platonist and nominalist debate on the nature and relationship of the universal and the particular. Suffice it to say here that particularity and universality are not a matter of either/or, but rather of both/and. The two aspects are two sides of the same coin as far as our perception of reality goes. In a class of only one member of humanity, the particular member would also be the universal, all in one. This reality does not change even when the class "humanity" has many members with differing accidental qualities. The difference is only a more colorful universal. The universal human character is realized by individuals maintaining the integrity of their lives in relation to one another under Christ, who is the bearer of authentic humanity. Therefore, to be human in Africa is to acknowledge our racial, cultural, historical, and sexual particularities and our commitment to human integrity as manifested in Jesus. To emphasize the universal at the expense of the particular leaves a distorted view of our humanity, as does the reverse.

Theoretical doctrinal abstraction that seek to maintain some universal essence without regard for historical particularity only helps to divorce theological thought from lived experience. By insisting on human universality, Mbiti falls victim to this error.

Jesus enters our culture and lives his life in it while he redeems and liberates it in order to imbue it with the values of his reign. Culture, though significant to our identity, cannot have finality because it is not absolute, but relative. It is not changeless, but changes. All aspects of culture that are liberative so as to engender development towards full human integrity have to be cultivated, while those that are oppressive of groups and of persons have to be abandoned in view of the call of Christ to an abundant life of integrity.[49] No oppression need be maintained in the name of culture. I indeed agree with Mbiti that our only authentic identity is with Christ, but in contrast to him, I insist that this identity is manifested in our particularity-universality continuum as black African people in one single historical existence. Mbiti's assertion that we must be first Christians and then Africans brings in a distinction that should not occur. Such a hierarchical distinction also brings into question the fact of incarnation. We have to be either Africans-in- Christ or simply Africans-without-Christ.

Foreign Terms and African Reality

One of his most vehement critics on Mbiti's use of foreign categories was the late Okot p'Bitek. He accused Mbiti among other African scholars of dressing African deities in hellenist robes.[50] The other African scholar who has been critical of Mbiti on this score is Gabriel Setiloane, late professor of African Religious Studies at the University of Cape Town. Setiloane criticizes Mbiti for not being critical enough of Western categories of thought and for not delving deep enough into African religious conceptions.[51] While not in complete agreement with p'Bitek and Setiloane, my own criticism centers on Mbiti's inadequate suspicion of some Western categories of thought, which he too easily accepted as normative in determining the essence of African religious thought. For instance, due to a lack of a comparable concept of eschatology, Mbiti reverses the western linear view of time and history and presents it as the African view. He states: "African peoples expect human history to continue forever, in the rhythm of moving from Sasa to Zamani and there is nothing to suggest that this rhythm will come to an end. . ."[52] The imposition of a western norm, even though reversed, has led Mbiti to deny the presence of salvation-history and a teleological aspect in African religions and history. Burleson also makes the same mistake by taking religion, history and salvation as used in the History of Religions School and applying them normatively to African religious reality leading to the erroneous conclusion that African religions are non-historical. This application of foreign norms, a view of history for Mbiti and a view of religion for Burleson, to African reality causes the two students of African culture to misrepresent African reality.

However, in fairness to Mbiti, this does not mean that foreign categories cannot be used. Academic disciplines tend to create a standard terminology of their own as their particular currency.[53] What is being criticized is a lack of a critical awareness in the application of these terminologies, some of which are culturally and historical determined in their meaning and may not carry the most appropriate connotations in a different historical and cultural milieu. By failing to keep a critical view, Mbiti failed at times to bring out the essential reality as experienced by the

Africans. For instance, while Mbiti does not develop a view of history, his denial of salvation-history in African religious tradition manifests the normative use of a western linear view of history and salvation which he applies to the African situation. A historically conscious people cannot fail to conceive of their own salvation as a people. In the study of African religions, history and culture, a norm by which all facts are to be organized needs to be discovered from within the study itself instead of imposing on the material some foreign norm thereby risking the distortion of African view of reality.

Salvation in African Historical Consciousness

Even though Mbiti rejects the idea of salvation-history, his writings speak of an experience that might be called Salvation-in-History. By this I mean a real, profound sense of God's saving activity among African people. Mbiti has clearly demonstrated this sense in one of his major works, *The Concepts of God in Africa*. After all, Paul reminds us that God has not left Godself without a witness; God's saving acts are an aspect of that witness. The reason for the rejection of salvation history, I suspect, lies in the way the term is used in relation to biblical salvation. Failing to find a comparable phenomenon, Mbiti concludes that such a phenomenon does not exist. The problem is that he is using the wrong measure.

In his article, "Some Reflections on African Experience of Salvation Today",[54] in which he recommendably seeks the essence of salvation in African experience, Mbiti states:

We might say from the start that many of the

practical expressions of African religion all over the
continent, are basically salvatory. ...They arise out
of man's need for help which comes from outside
his own abilities.[55]

Obviously Mbiti does not agree with Burleson's conception of non-
historical religions that place salvation outside of history. Mbiti
says that African religions are salvatory. Is it possible to have
salvation in African religion and not have the equivalent of
salvation-history?

God, as Mbiti maintains, is thought to be the ultimately
source of all means of salvation. There is, therefore and contrary
to Mbiti a salvation history that operates within the history of
African people in the context of the ontological relatedness
mentioned above. However, conceptually the African view differs
from the Christian view of salvation-history, in which God's
salvatory events enjoy high visibility and move towards an
anticipated consummation.[56] Mbiti observes that for many African
people, God's active participation in human history is seen in
terms of his supplying them with rain, good harvest, health,
children, and cattle.[57] Since Mbiti maintains a utilitarian view of
salvation in African religions and uses the Christian view as a
measuring rod, he does not see salvation-history in the former. In
my opinion, Mbiti does acknowledge a more diffused view of
salvation-history, which may be called Salvation-in-History. This
view of salvation fits into the historical consciousness of the
African people because it is concerned with both the historical and
ontological security and safety. What is paramount in this kind of
salvation is not salvation from the consequences of sin, but rather
human wellness. It is security from sickness, danger, and famine.

African Humanity and the Christian View of Salvation

Mbiti asks, how Jesus can be a firm point of reference and hold together the hopes embedded in traditional religion?[58] This question is both evangelical and Christological in character. It is evangelical in that it has to do with the goodness of the Goodnews of Jesus for the African people. It is Christological in that it implies the further question, Who is Jesus for the African people? Mbiti's concern is how African Christians perceive Jesus in the context of their religio-cultural milieu. This is an important matter for Mbiti in view of the numerical growth of Christianity in Sub-Saharan Africa and the consequent urgency for theological understanding and articulation of the faith. He wants to understand what Africans see and find in this Jesus to whom they are turning in such great numbers.

The faith of the African Christians is grounded and centered upon Jesus because in and through him, they have come to experience and know the power of God to save and protect from both human and cosmic forces. Jesus meets their present needs for spiritual and physical security and gives them power to deal with the spiritual forces that they have struggled against for a long time. Jesus is seen as the concentration of divine power. Through the incarnation, God becomes visible and a tangible point to which one can run for refuge. Jesus represents the almightiness of God. Therefore Jesus means salvation/liberation from forces of death to abundant life. The incarnation humanizes Jesus so that he becomes one with us. Jesus becomes one with us in order to perfect both persons and cultures. While Mbiti maintains that it is the culture which surrenders first to Christ, and thereby surrendering humanity to him, I think that the reverse is the case. When persons surrender to Christ, they perpetuate the incarnation of Jesus which is made concrete in their lives by the agency of the indwelling Holy Spirit, thereby effecting change in the culture. This order fits with Jesus' declaration to the disciples that they were the salt of the earth and the light of the world.[59] By being salt and light, they were the means to humanize society and to bring light to it.

African Christians see in Jesus also the meaning of human wholeness. Jesus is viewed as the perfect human being who has gone through similar rites of passage and thus fulfills everything that constitutes the wholesomeness of corporate living.[60] Mbiti has witnessed some aspects of what has come to be known as the East African Revival. One mark of the people's encounter with the reality of Jesus has been joy and a sense of newness of life. It is this experience which makes the gospel personally goodnews and is crucial to the doing of theology. This is one reason why theology for him "arises out of the spontaneous joy in being a Christian, responding to life and ideas as one redeemed."[61] Therefore, theology cannot be detached from a personal experience and relationship with Christ. It arises out of and is a function of one's discipleship and witness to Jesus' saving presence in one's life and in the world.

According to Mbiti, in African religious perspective the Christological title of savior has physical and moral, but not eschatological connotations. This understanding is in keeping with the African concept of salvation in which saving is a constant event. Since for Mbiti savior has no future connotation in terms of salvation, this view also fits well with African conception of time which lacks a teleological end. However, it is the reality of Christ, especially his resurrection, which introduces and makes concrete for the African Christians the eschatological dimension of both personal and historical teleology. Yet God's revelation in Christ is not totally discontinuous with traditional African beliefs, Mbiti argues. He supports his argument by referring to the timelessness of Jesus as a result of the resurrection.[62] Jesus cannot be limited to one time and place. This argument is impressive, but far fetched. Again, had Mbiti recognized the future dimension of time in African thought, the question of continuity or discontinuity would not have arisen at all. The fulfillment Jesus brings would not be perceived in terms of time but in terms of quality of eschatological vision and sense of being. It is because of the quality of the eschatological vision and the present experience of a dynamic sense of well being in association with Jesus as the great *Ng'anga* (meaning healer, perhaps the closest Bantu word equivalent to Christ as a Christological title) that many Africans are turning to Jesus.

Jesus is a universal event that accommodates itself to all localities yet   confines itself to none. Jesus summons human culture to a higher moral plane by making his own transcended life come to bear on humanity. For Mbiti, Jesus is human, but his ascension makes him transcendent. Mbiti, therefore, espouses a form of adoptionist Christology. But while it is necessary to distinguish between what is human and what is divine, we must not forget that an ontological relationship obtains between the two. This ontological relationship implies that since human beings as created are humanly divine, Jesus as God incarnate was also humanly divine. The resurrection reveals the full cosmic nature of Jesus as being also spiritually divine; it does not establish it as Mbiti maintains. We can avoid the Christological heresies if we grant an ontological relationship between the divine and the human, between the immanent and the transcendent, because they imply and are fulfilled by each other. I submit that authentic humanity as manifested in Jesus is also divinity. To be divinized in Christ is to be authentically humanized; that is the meaning of salvation and/or of "inheriting the reign of God." The reign of God manifests itself concretely by its values of love, justice and mercy, service and truth. A divinized humanity proves itself by exhibiting the values of the reign of God. Jesus came not only to fulfill African culture but much more the creators of African culture so that they may attain to authentic humanity. This is the fulfillment of the African sense of salvation and should constitute the meaning of salvation in Africa today.

In the next chapter I will show how a Christian doctrine of humanity can be worked out so as to take full advantage of the insights of African culture and present reality. It has to be a doctrine that is centered in the reality of Jesus as one who fulfills African vision of authentic humanity as realized in the reign of God. This involves the restoration of the cosmic role for humanity which was disturbed and thereby securing harmony. Jesus has secured the possibility of that harmony and it is in relation with him that human beings enter into that role again. It is not through the concept of time.

CHAPTER SEVEN

UMUNTHU:
TOWARD AN AFRICAN CHRISTIAN ANTHROPOLOGY

Since time is one of the natural givens that human beings can do little to alter, the dictum, "I am because we are, and since we are, therefore, I am," serves as a most suitable key or heuristic tool for understanding African ontology, philosophy, and religion than time does. Time, however, will always remain the context in which life is lived and philosophy and religion practiced.

While Mbiti restricts the dictum, "I am because we are, and since we are, therefore, I am," to the explanation of kinship and the African communitarian ethos, its application as a philosophical, religious and cultural principle needs to be extended to explain also the historical and cosmic interrelatedness of beings. This interrelated reality, which I call **ontological/Life Relationality**, is foundational to the personal, communal, historical and cosmic consciousness of African peoples. The essential import of the dictum embraces this totality.

Ontological/Life Relationality

Life relationality is expressed by a holistic way of knowing called **ontological/life cognition.** Life cognition includes rationality, feelings, faith, doubt, imagination, consciousness, wisdom, and all experience, and it aims at totality of impression and expression. There is a diffuseness about life cognition that occurs precisely because the whole conscious-self with its depths of unconsciousness is involved. It is this diffuseness that becomes the raw material for reason which gets focus on any given aspect of it for greater clarity. In this life cognition, there is more than only one type of logic that operates. There is a multiple logical systems operate relationally in different ways and at different levels. This logical multiplicity is made meaningful only by our human consciousness in a cultural context. Each individual person becomes a center of integration and communication of all that experience and the concomitant knowledge. Such a multiplicity of levels of knowledge is a more accurate description of cognition because life is not static, but dynamic; and not simple, but complex, always in a state of becoming. To the knower, the known has no independent existence except in and through conscious appropriation and objectification. This cognitive experience fits well into an understanding of humanity in which humanization is an on-going process throughout a person's life rooted within a multi-dimensional network of relationships.

This humanizing process——being human by always becoming human,——does not apply only to individuals. The whole community is also supposed to be a human and humanizing community moving toward the goal of realizing the **Good Village or Community**. The humanizing processes are meant to foster rightly related individuals and communities. In order to achieve this goal, humanity summons the help of as many cosmic forces as it can to fight off evil forces that threaten personal, communal, and cosmic harmony. The good community and cosmic harmony are the foundational goals of rites of passage.

The humanizing process as a manifestation of ontological relationality demands mutual relationships in which each person is able to develop a morally righteous (humanly authentic) character and is able to contribute economically. Character and economic productivity are the indices of human integrity and authenticity. Mutuality eschews domination; only through mutuality can a responsible human community emerge. Only this kind of individual can truly be a cosmic priest to God and a member of a community that becomes a Good Village (holy nation) by striving towards being truly human.

Toward an African Theological Anthropology

Christian teaching on humanity came to Africa with the missionaries in a prepackaged doctrinal and cultural form. It was meant to be adopted whole without regard to the local views and what they could offer. However, the imported doctrine of humanity——based on the truth that all people are made in the image of God and are loved by God for redemption in spite of themselves——was not matched by the messengers' practice especially in their view and treatment of the African people. I have come to believe that the validity of any theological system depends not only on its logical and theological coherence but even more the way that truth is embodied by those who claim it. It is false theology to claim that all people are made in the image of God and then live to oppress a whole people just because they were created black or women or because they did not discover and manufacture both guns and gunpowder in time to conquer and dominate. Divorcing doctrine from ethics and subjugating both to racial superiority distorted not only the doctrine of God but the doctrine of humanity as well. Past and anticipated future distortions of this nature emphasize the need for the Church in Africa to be theologically responsible to itself.

Thus far, African theology has been searching for

theological method(s) as it attempts to define itself and its agenda. Many studies on doctrinal issues have been essentially comparative seeking to establish bridges between African and Christian/biblical religious thought. In what I consider a second stage of his theological creativity, Mbiti is attempting to construct African Christian theology by synthesizing traditional African and biblical thought. It is my conviction that the theological task now must move toward more constructive systematic work. Abundant data and resources for this work have been collected in articles, dissertations and books. The task must also become more inclusive by claiming the insights of all African peoples as African insights.

An African doctrine of Christian anthropology will take into account the cultural, socio-economic, political, and historical understanding of humanity in addition to the biblical data in order to formulate a relevant doctrine that will shape the psycho-spiritual, religious, and socio-politico-economic attitudes and practices of African Christians in particular, and the African public in general, presently and in the immediate future.

Such a doctrine concerning humanness must be intentionally both pragmatic and programmatic, not abstract. It must be pragmatic in order to deal with our historical and cultural existence as the concrete expression of our essential Africanness. It must be programmatic so as to set forth a style of life that has human well being (salvation/liberation) as its major concern, otherwise the doctrine will lack existential meaning and relevance. I will delineate below some major contours of what I consider to be a relevant, pragmatic, and programmatic doctrine of humanness. This doctrinal framework is provisional in nature. It remains to be developed, but that is another book.

Humanness is the Image of God

The African myths of creation corroborated by the biblical narratives are clear about the ultimate transcendent origin of human beings. By virtue of being created by God, human beings are children of God. This double relationship to God as both creature and child can be fully appreciated only when both terms are given full weight. Being a child of God is related to the biblical concept of humanity being made in the image of God.[1] The concept of ontological relationality encompasses this transcendental relationship that is fundamental to human self-definition. With an awareness of these two dimensions of our relationship to God, that is, our creatureliness and childhood, comes consciousness of a dignity and an integrity (Humanness) that is exclusively human. In my African society, this thought is usually stated negatively. To object to any infringement on one's dignity as a human being, a person will always contend that he/she is not a beast or animal to be treated thus. It is thought that to ill-treat someone is to regard them as an animal, a beast of burden.[2] An objection to this negative view of oneself is a recognition and assertion that one's dignity as a human being needs to be recognized. The idea of humanness connotes a character of integrity, and so it negates any corrupt human character. It is an idea used to condemn all that is unbecoming, evil, and a betrayal of that moral integrity that is essentially human. A failure to manifest this humanness reduces one to the level of a beast with a human face.

To be human means more than just the physical shape or

form of a human being. The glory that is human has to be expressed concretely in order to be realized by oneself and acknowledged by others. Evil and shameful actions tarnish and diminish one's sense of dignity and integrity. Such actions can be self-generated or done to one by others. This happens when one abdicates the socially acceptable sense of human dignity and integrity, or simply, humanness. In other words, when we act unwisely, we affect the quality of our humanness so strongly that we turn it into that of a brutish animal driven by instinct. This reversal of our behavior is what marks most concretely our fallenness. Such a fall from humanness into inhumanity is therefore, a fall away from God's authentic image. In the biblical narrative, when Adam and Eve realized their nakedness, they had lost their dignity. They found themselves in a state of utter humiliation brought on by their own action. This loss of dignity and integrity marked the condition of our fallen humanity: a life of contradiction and a divided existence.

Our humanness is relational; and to maintain such relationship positively, we need wisdom. Wisdom is the choosing the right means for the right ends with a view to maintaining human harmony and well being. A wisdom tradition of proverbs, fables, myths, parable, wise sayings, and all kinds of stories are very prevalent in African societies as aids in acquiring wisdom upon which right relationships are established. Humanness as the expression of the image of God in us translates itself into relationships characterized by integrity and wisdom.

Reconciled Person-in-Community and Communion

In order to recapture our human dignity, integrity, and

wisdom, we do not primarily need an education; rather we need a reconciliation to our essential humanity. This reconciliation to our essential humanness is a process through which we get reconciled to the total universe. To be human in Africa is to be a reconciled person-in-community-and-communion responsibly living out the integrity of one's humanness in all spheres of life and thus contributing to the development and realization of what we have called the Good Village or Community and harmony in the cosmos. It is to be "I am because we are, and since we are, therefore, I am." Such reconciliation becomes even more significant as we recognize and acknowledge the perpetual reversal of our humanness, whereby we become alienated from ourselves, from others, from God, from our environment, and the spirit world. This existential condition of alienness is what Oscar Bimwenyi-Kweshi has described as fugitiveness, a feeling of not being at home, a condition of wandering about because one is lost and perpetually searching for a life that lasts.[3] In this condition human meaning is greatly diminished; it is essentially a state of destitution. As Engelbert Mveng has asserted, we are the divided persons who divide the world.[4] As has already been pointed out, such a state might be partly self-inflicted and partly due to other people within or without one's community.

Mbiti has asserted that African myths do not provide a way out of this alienation from the cosmic community. It is not surprising then that God the creator must take the initiative to reverse that backward trend on our behalf, thus effecting reconciliation that is most unusual because it is entirely the result of God's grace and reconstituting us into a *koinonia* (Community-in-Communion). Community-in-Communion has always been

African peoples' ideal state of being; part of the purpose of rites
of passage is to help toward this end. In Christ and through the
regenerating agency of the Holy Spirit God is able to accomplish
this reconciliation in and among us.

To be human is not only to belong to a community as a
responsible member but also to have communion, which is the
mark of a reconciled community. Communion is mutually
nurturing, open, and vibrant relationships. Concretely, it means
mutual availability to one another, a share in material well-being,
and the speaking of a word that builds up community.[5] It is
sharing in the flow of a common life and common spirit of
goodwill in the community. This communion extends to the spirits
of the departed and, with them, to God. As Emmanuel Twesigye
points out, "[T]he human community is also the divine arena of
the human beings' own creation, socialization or humanization..."[6]
We live in a related universe and it is a fundamentally religious
vocation.

The New Testament metaphor of the church as body
reflects an organic relationality close to the way African
communities understand themselves.   The Church as the
community of redeemed humanness is the new society; it is the
new being made manifest and becomes in turn an agent of
humanization (or redemption). The church can accomplish this
vocation only in union and communion with Christ. The church
has this tremendous kerygmatic and discipling task, the task of
continually evangelizing and initiating people into the mysteries of
the new humanity in Christ as they live their lives as witnesses in
the world. In this task word and action so complement each other
that one cannot be conceived without the other. The church of the

new humanity does not separate itself physically, but remains in the community as salt and light. It is empowered within the community so that all may benefit. However, the historical reality of the Church as a fragmented body, a body apart from the African community and living impatiently within it, provides a miserably poor paradigm for restoring African societies to the ideal of humanness. The African church must overcome its divisions in order to be truly the church of authentic humanity today.

Many Peoples, but One Humanity

To be human is to accept one's ethnic, cultural, and historical identity as a gift from God and a communal contribution to the mosaic of ethnicities and cultures in the world in a spirit of openness, tolerance, and appreciation of what is different. While African societies tended to be ethnocentric, the Gospel of the new humanity in Christ calls for removal of the dividing walls of hostility and creation of the one humanity.[7] Ethnically, people become dehumanized by being discriminated against, marginalized, and dominated and also by dominating. They become dehistoricized by being landless, culturally uprooted, homeless, and jobless. So, for example, refugees are a deeply theological issue; as refugees people are unable to relate to their ethnic environment, especially the land, culture and creative work, thereby being robbed of some important aspects of their humanity. Discrimination and domination on whatever grounds are sacriligious because human ethnic, cultural, and historical identity are sacred gifts from God and for God. They are the extension of our being made in the image of God and they must be protected at any cost. Being gifts, they have no ultimate significance in and of themselves apart from God. To absolutize them as means of excluding other people from the blessing of God invests them with ultimate significance and is a form of idolatry. In Jesus, we are meant to become and we do indeed become one large, multi-ethnic, extended family, clan, nation, and race of humanity. Therefore, walls of exclusion must give way to a new relationship in the new humanity in Christ. This new humanity is the expression of the church universal, yet it is always particularly located. United by the same spirit of life in which we all participate, everyone has the priestly function and responsibility to see to it that the right sacrifices of humane attitudes and actions are offered. The implications for Africa are obvious. Tribalism, racism, sexism, classism, regionalism, and all other isms, even ideological Christianity, that would claim ultimate control over our being become evils that threaten our new humanity in Christ.

Living Toward Full Humanness

To be human in African is a process of being by becoming. It is living and growing towards full humanness, a process that is also prefigured in the rites of passage. The goal of authentic humanity translates into being mature and responsible as a human being after the model of Christ. The very heart of Christian discipleship is living and growing toward the "whole measure of the fullness of Christ,"[8] who embodies in himself that full humanness. Mature humanhood is defined not only by legal age, physical development, educational and professional attainment or reproductive processes, but much more by wisdom expressed in the best possible ways of relating so that community and communion are strengthened. Therefore, mature humanhood rejects any alliance with forces of chaos and death on the one hand, and cooperates with all forces that work for abundant life on the other. It is said of Jesus that "he grew in wisdom and stature, and in favor with God and men."[9] This is what "to be human" means. To do so, one must relate well to all and to be that kind of person takes a lot of discipline and wisdom. Unfortunately, this emphasis on wisdom has been sacrificed on the altar of western education. It must be noted, to our shame, that both African traditional societies and especially the church as the supposed new society of the new humanity are always poor approximations to genuine humanness, which has been made manifest in Jesus and can be embodied only in association with him. For African traditional societies, humans' inability to live out their own concept of humanness is clear evidence that they live under the power of sin from which only Jesus can rescue them. The church's poor showing in carrying out Jesus' full humanness stems from unfaithfulness.[10] The church needs urgently to repent of this unfaithfulness so that it can be renewed by the Holy Spirit, the Spirit of our regeneration. When professional and academic development and achievements are wrongly made substitutes for growth in humanness, our humanness remains stunted for lack of appropriate nurture. One is never too old for this kind of growth; to be human is to manifest a deep desire to grow towards the ultimate goal of humanness. To be like Christ is to reach the point of maturation.

Created in Freedom for Freedom

To be human in Africa means to be individually and communally free to determine for oneself and as a corporate body the quality of life within the given natural constraints.[11] So to live is to cast a vote for genuine freedom against fear of political repercussions, oppression, exploitation, domination, and exclusion in the name of culture, national security, and political expedience. Jean-Marc Ela has expressed this point even more succinctly by saying,

> Now, if the glory of God never demands the human
> being's mutilation, then it is the task of
> Christians to discover and manifest a faith in Christ that
> does not dispense the human being from the
> obligation to be a free, responsible subject.[12]

This sense of freedom does not need to translate into individualism at the expense of community. Without freedom, communion, and therefore also community, is impossible. The elevation of the individual at the expense of the communal spirit only results into rugged individualism which would dehumanize both individual and community. Yet, freedom is for the expression and development of individuality. Even though the African is a person-in-community, more space needs to be created for more individual initiative and contribution for the enrichment of the total community. This means that freedoms of expression, association, choice of political parties, and economic enterprise are fundamental to the realization of authentic humanity in African today. Freedom does not mean license and has nothing to do with license. Freedom is a product of love and is responsible. License in the name of freedom is counterfeit and must be exposed to be such. License is an enemy of humanness.

Political challenges to humanness in Africa take the form

not only of apartheid South Africa, but also of single party dictatorships which rule by fear generated by a few privileged people supported by capitalist weapons and money at the expense of the ordinary rural and working class people. The true index of freedom and responsibility of any government is improvement in the quality of life of the poor and the governments accountability to them as citizens. Claiming that national security must be strengthened to assure the momentum of development, many of these single party dictatorships and military regimes become very oppressive towards their own people. As Ela asserts, "In the task of development, not just our work is engaged, but also our becoming, our genesis. By transforming the conditions of our life we attain to our full humanity."[13] Therefore, oppression and development cannot be carried out by the same regime. It is a contradiction in terms. Freedom is very fundamental to the process of development; it is not limited to the political realm, but extends to all aspects of human existence—economic, mental, social, cultural, religious. Africa has a long way to go in realizing even a semblance of freedom for the majority of its population.

Development should not be seen in material terms only. Rather, material development should be assessed in terms of who benefits, at whose expense. Authentic humanity implies freedom to be by becoming human. Freedom is imperilled whenever people begin to relate badly politically, socially, economically, and even religiously. Power of whatever kind is for service and not control. To be a leader is to become a donkey for the others to ride, not to turn others into donkeys for the leader to ride. When power is used for service and the empowerment of the powerless it nourishes and strengthens freedom. However, when power is used to control and dominate, it undermines freedom and humanness. As the apostle Paul tells us, love is God's way of controlling the community of the new humanity;[14] love is the way of authentic humanness.

A Culture of Liberation

It has been underscored above that to be human includes being culturally free and creative. Yet in the name of culture, not only men but primarily women and children are cultural captives. In many societies, women and children are treated as the human property of their fathers, husbands and brothers for the males commercial benefit. Without something like a prophetic tradition that serves as an internal self-critique of a given society, culture becomes a primary tool of oppression and enslavement, especially when it takes on religious overtones. A community with more than half of its members under cultural servitude is itself in bondage and ignorant of humanness; such a community is impoverished by such bondage. The church itself has misconstrued the biblical views on women by stifling what God is saying through women (usually called "exceptional" women) when they do speak and/or act powerfully in the name of God. It never occurs to the church that God's spirit may be breaking the traditional boundaries to which the Spirit has been limited. The church has found it easy to say that all are made in the image of God while treating some (women especially) as if they were not. But what defines a person is the way that person is treated, not simply what the Bible says applied abstractly.

While Africa is seeking its cultural liberation, it must at the same time liberate women from the oppressive aspects of African culture. Engelbert Mveng has touched on a very significant and fundamental point for African humanity when he asserts that "the African woman is not a problem, but a solution to all the problems." He elaborates:

> This does not mean that she has no problems. To be a solution to other people's problems is to be the target for all the problems; it is literally to carry the weight of all problems. A close look at the traditional society and at the anthropology which forms its basis shows that woman, being the necessary second[15]dimension of the human person, represents the victory of life over death. That is why she may be said to be the solution to all problems. ...We can, at the very least, guess why maternity and the ministry of life in all its ritualistic expression best represents the feminine function in traditional Africa.[16]

It is, therefore, no light matter when Mercy Oduyoye insists that Feminism in Africa is a precondition for Christian anthropology.[17] If liberation means anything, then it must be liberation for all, leading to servanthood by all under the lordship of Jesus, the true servant.

A Christian doctrine of humanity must expose all structural aspects of cultural oppression as part of the role of the gospel to redeem individuals and cultures. Jesus makes it very clear that certain biblical positions were actually concessions made due to the hardness of people's hearts.[18] Paul did not prove an exception to this practice either.[19] In addition, there is a biblical mandate for the church to bind and unbind practices. All these precedents give the African church ample room to deal with matter that have been used to oppress and marginalize some in the name of God's word while it was simply patriarchy on the throne.

Creating and Maintaining Humane Structures

To be human is to order life in community according to humane structures. Inhumane structures correlate directly to bad relationships between people, either as individuals or as economic, social, and even language groups. The creation of just socio-economic and political structures locally, nationally, and internationally would go a long way to help African people move towards the realization of authentic humanity.

Ela's analysis that the source of structural inhumanity in Africa is dependent development as opposed to autonomous development is partly right. In dependent development, relationships are characterized by domination and exploitation; while in autonomous development relationships are based on liberation and self-actualization.[20] Structures have got to be adapted to respond to human needs for quality living and not left to develop a life of their own or controlled by one interest group to the impoverishment of other groups. If, as Jesus said, the sabbath is made for the good of human beings and not human beings for the sabbath,[21] then, no institution may be allowed to make human beings its servants or slaves, be that institution political or cultural. Institutions are for the good of humanity, not humanity for the good of institutions, in disregard of the quality of their own lives. It needs to be said, however, that personal sin cannot be entirely divorced from structural and institutional evil without making societal structures merely scapegoats. Personal and societal evil are two sides of the same coin. They are to be reckoned together and face squarely if humanness is to be realized.

The Cosmic Temple and its Duties

To be human in Africa is to be in priestly service in the cosmic temple in which every act, word, or thought should be a sweet-smelling offering to God and to all humanity, living or departed. African humanity cannot dispense with its religiosity without also losing part of itself. Western Christianity, in spite of its own foundations, has tended to compartmentalize life, so that religion is only an aspect of life. As a result, for many people the practice of Christianity is only liturgical and not existential. African spirituality is cosmic and expresses itself in the total flow of life towards other beings and realities. Humanness is the practice of good religion; such practice casts a vote against bad religion, which is everything that dehumanizes. Witchcraft, discrimination, nepotism, corruption, violence, and foolishness are all aspects of bad religion. To live is to be religious. To be religious is to be ontologically related.

Since Christ, who is the image of the invisible God, has manifested authentic humanity in an ultimate way, it is only in relationship with him that good religion is possible, because through him we attain to authentic humanness ontologically and existentially. That is, the ideal becomes manifested on the historical plane. Therefore, the *praeparatio evangelica* consists not only in African culture, but also in the self-understanding of the African people and their consciousness of the dignity and integrity that is human. Yet the full reality of this humanness remains hidden until one encounters Jesus. The Gospel as the humanizing agent has to be interlocked to this self- and cultural understanding in order to result in an authentically African Christian anthropology. Those who are committed to the realization of authentic human integrity or genuine humanness are the ones who truly humanize cultures, societal structures and institutions, and the world. These are the ones who truly inherit the earth and realize the reign of God.

It is with this understanding of Christ's mission that Mbiti is right on target when he says, "But only Christianity has the terrible responsibility of pointing the way to that ultimate Identity, Foundation and Source of security."[22] This is the challenge of the African church. It has to put its own house in order not only theologically, but practically if it is to contribute effectively to the salvation and liberation of African people. God help the church! God bless Africa! Amen.

NOTES

CHAPTER ONE

1. Humanness is the rendering of the following in some of the languages of Malawi: *umunthu* in Chichewa, *unthu* in Chitumbuka, *ubundu* in Chindali). All these ethnic groups converge on the centrality of this idea of humanness in their educational and cultural philosophy.

2. Nyasaland, Malawi's colonial name, became a British protectorate in 1891 as part of the process of partitioning Africa generated by the Berlin Conference of 1884 and became Malawi on attainment of independence in 1964.

3. Harvey Sindima, "Community of Life," in *The Ecumenical Review*, 41, No. 4, (1989): pp. 537-551. In this article, Dr. Sindima traces the conception of a mechanistic worldview as far back as 400 BCE to Democritus and shows have it has been developed since in the West as the dominant view.

4. Both Senghor and Nyerere were the first presidents of their respective countries and are both in retirement.

5. I have in mind here Engelbert Mveng of Cameroon and Oscar Bimwenyi Kweshi of Zaire, who have addressed the matter of theological anthropology from an African perspective. See E. Mveng, *l'Afrique dans l'Eglise Paroles d'un Croyant*. Paris: l'Harmattan, 1985; "African Liberation Theology" in Leonardo Boff and Virgil Elizondo, *Theologies of the Third World*. Edinburg: T & T Clark Ltd., 1988. pp. 17-34; "Third World Theology--What Theology? What Third World?: An Evaluation of an African Delegate." In Virginia Fabella and Sergio Torres, *Irruption of the Third World: Challenge to Theology*. Maryknoll, New York: Orbis Books, 1983. pp. 217-221; Oscar Bimwenyi-Kweshi, *Discours Theologique Negro-Africaine*. Paris: Presence Africaine, 1981.

6. Perhaps the leading African feminist theologian is Mercy Amba Oduyoye, formerly of Ibadan University and currently a deputy secretary of the World Council of Churches. Her book *Hearing and Knowing*, (Maryknoll, New York: Orbis, 1986), has a challenging chapter on "Feminism: A Precondition for Christian Anthropology," pp. 120-137. She has many other articles to her credit. Oduyoye and other African women, Rosemary Edet, Rosemary Nithamburi and Rose Zoe Obianga, just to name some, are active in the Ecumenical Association of Third World Theologians and the continental Ecumenical Association of African Theologians. Through these associations, their voices are going to be heard more and more within Africa and far beyond.

7. Mbiti, "A Change of the African Concept of Man Through Christian Influence," in Gnana Robinson, ed., *For the Sake of the Gospel*, (Arasaradi, Mudurai: T.T.S. Publications,1980) p.56.

8. This ontological difference is underscored by what the Fang of Cameroun say: "Nzame (God) is on high, man is below! Nzame is Nzame, man is man: Each to himself, each in his dwelling." Mbiti, "Man in African Religion," in Isaac James Mowoe and Richard Bjornson, eds., *Africa and the West, the Legacies of Empire*, (New York: Greenwood Press, 1986). p. 57.

CHAPTER TWO

1. John Mbiti, "African Indigenous Culture in Relation to Evangelism and Church Development" in R. Pierce Beaver, ed., *The Gospel and Frontier Peoples*, (Pasadena, California: William Carey Library, 1973), pp.79-95.

2. Mbiti, "New Testament Eschatology and the Akamba of Kenya" in David Barrett, ed., *African Initiatives in Religion*, (Nairobi: East African Publishing House, 1971), p.18.

3. Mbiti, "Hope, Time and Christian Hope" in *Lumen Vitae*, Vol. XXX, No. 1 (1975), p. 103.

5. James Emman Kwegyir Aggrey was born in 1875 at Anamabu in Ghana. In 1898, he sailed to the United States of America in pursuit of further education (as did many who were to be leaders in Africa). After an eventful stay in America, he returned to West Africa with a Ph.D from Columbia University and a B.D. from Union Theological Seminary. The name of Aggrey became known throughout Africa as a result of his appointment twice as a member of the Phelps-Stock Commission, 1921 and 1923. The Commission had the task of evaluating the appropriateness of African education. In 1921 the Commission visited West and South Africa and in 1923 the Commission visited East Africa. The presence of Aggrey in that delegation was an inspiration to many aspiring young black people all over Africa. I can remember Agrrey's name being mentioned in the 1950s with fondness and admiration as though he had just visited.

6. Mbiti alludes to the story in his article, "Theological Impotence and the Universality of the Church" in Gerald Anderson and Thomas Stransky, eds. *Mission Trends No.3, Third World Theologies*, (Ramsay, N.J. and Grand Rapids, Mi.: Paulist/Eerdmans, 1976), p.13. In a personal interview on June 9th, 1989 at Burgdorf, Switzerland, he elaborated further on this momentous event in his life.

7. The thesis was published in part under the title, *New Testament Eschatology in an African Background*, (London: Oxford University Press, 1971).

8. "The Encounter of Christian Faith and African Religion" in *The Christian Century*, Vol. XCVII, No. 27 (Aug. 27- Sept. 3, 1980) p. 818.

9. Ibid., p. 817.

10. Mbiti, "The Encounter of Christian Faith and African Religion," op. cit., p. 817.

11. Ibid., p. 819.

12. Ibid., p. 819.

13. Mbiti, "Division or Unity?" in *One World*, No.3 (Feb.1975), p.13.

14. By the term "geography of salvation," Mbiti means places sacred to different church group regarded as such. Palestine is not the only Holy Land. There are others. For instance, the Kimbanguists regard the village of N'Kamba as a sacred site where a holy pool is located. He writes, "Jesus is savior of the world and the world is both history and geography." *Bible and Theology in African Christianity*, op. cit., p.171.

15. Mbiti, "The Encounter of Christian Faith and African Religion," op. cit., p. 819.

16. Mbiti, *New Testament Eschatology*, op. cit., p. 106.

17. See also John Macquarrie, "The Anglican Theological Tradition" in Richard Holloway, ed., *The Anglican Tradition*, (London: Mowbray, 1984), pp.17-34; Peter Toon, *The Anglican Way*, (Wilton, Conn.: Morehouse-Barlow Co., 1983.)

18. Kwame Bediako, "Identity and Integration: An Inquiry into the Nature and Problems of Theological Indigenization in Selected Early Hellenistic and Modern African Christian Writers," doctoral dissertation presented to the University of Aberdeen (1983), (henceforth referred to as *Identity and Integration*). p. 380.

19. According to his unpublished bibliography, the article "Christianity Is Replacing Native Religions in Africa" appeared in *Presence Africaine*, No. 11 (Aug. - Nov. 1959). This article may not be the first one. A note in the bibliography which Mbiti compiled points to the fact that there are articles written between 1955 and 1963 that cannot be traced.

20.. He later went on to become professor and head of the department. The British nomenclature for university position is hierarchical. At the lower end is the Assistant Lecturer, then

195

Lecturer, Senior Lecturer, Reader, and, at the top is Professor.

21. The poem "Gethsemane" ends with these words, "Down an angel came/ To strengthen and comfort give/ In solitary Gethsemane/ Where Christ triumphs/ Over death and life." (Nairobi: East African Publishing House, 1969), p.49.

22. *Love and Marriage in Africa*, (London: Longman, 1973), Preface.

23. Mbiti, *Prayers of African Religion*, (London: SPCK, 1975).

24. Mbiti, Ibid., p. 13.

25. Mbiti, *African Religions and Philosophy*, op. cit., p. 1.

26. Bediako, *Identity and Integration*, op. cit., (1983), p. 389. Kwame Bediako is right to see a theologically informed purpose running through the three works. I will come back to this in its appropriate place further on.

27. The books he has edited include, *African and Asian Contributions to Contemporary Theology*, (Bossey, Switzerland: Ecumenical Institute, 1977); *Confessing Christ in Different Cultures*, (Bossey. Switzerland: Ecumenical Institute, 1977); *Christian and Jewish Dialogue on Man*, (Bossey, Switzerland: Ecumenical Institute, 1980); *Indigenous Theology and the Universal Church*, (Bossey, Switzerland: Ecumenical Institute 1979).

28. Gerald Anderson and Thomas Stransky, ed, *Mission Trends No. 3: Third World Theologies*, op. cit., (1976). This article first appeared in the *Lutheran World*, XXI/3, (1974).

29. Ibid., p.8

30.. Mbiti cites Paul Tillich as manifesting this attitude when he advised, as late as 1959 in his *Theology of Culture* (ed. R.C. Kimball, (New York: Oxford University Press, 1959), that "what

196

we do with primitive peoples in the mission field" should be the same as what he advises to be done with children, namely: "Ye seek to answer their questions and in doing so we, at the same time, slowly transform their existence so that they come to ask the questions to which the christian message gives the answer."(p.206) What Tillich has done, Mbiti charges, is to give a theological imprimatur to this negative attitude.

31. Mbiti, "African indigenous Cultures in Relation to Evangelism and Church Development," in R. Pierce Beaver, ed., *The Gospel and Frontier Peoples*, op. cit., (1973). p. 82.

32. Ibid., p. 82.

33. The conference papers were published as a book under the title, *African Theology en Route*, by Orbis in 1979. The same article in a slightly edited form appears as chapter three of Mbiti's book, *Bible and Theology in African Christianity*, (Nairobi: Oxford University Press, 1986). (henceforth, *Bible and Theology*) It is from this book that the above reference is taken. See p.59.

34. Kofi Appiah-Kubi and Sergio Torres, eds. *African Theology en Route*, op. cit., (1979). p. 192.

35. Mbiti, *Bible and Theology*, op.cit., p. 60.

36. Mbiti, "Some African Concepts of Christology" in Georg Vicedom, ed., *Christ and the Younger Churches*, (London: S.P.C.K., 1972), pp. 51-62.

37. Mbiti may seem, here, to be accommodating to and uncritical of the racial, cultural and even national bias of the dominant theology. Perhaps he should employ a hermeneutic of suspicion. While he is aware of some of these shortcomings, he does not intend either to throw out the theological baby with the bath-water or accept the whole tradition uncritically. Rather, he would have the theological tradition recast in an African form, not by way of adaptation but through fecundity. The adaptation approach advocates a process of substituting certain western concepts for

African ones while fecundity implies a fusion of two different elements into a new reality.

38. Mbiti, *New Testament Eschatology*, op. cit., p. 189.

39. In the interpretation of the history of early Christianity, the proliferation of religious and philosophical groups and symptoms of spiritual hunger that they represented, the *Pax Romana*, the Roman highways, widely spoken languages, business enterprises, and a common civilization were all viewed as a propitious factors for the Gospel. It was a divine preparation for the effective communication of the Gospel. Mbiti's question is, Why limit this understanding of history to the Roman Empire only? Why not extend it to all peoples, especially those in Africa where the growth of Christianity has been phenomenal and unprecedented? For him, if there is a significant factor equal to the *Pax Romana*, it is the *Religio Africana*. Therefore, the study of African traditional religion must be taken seriously indeed. Just as one cannot understand early Christianity without an adequate knowledge of the Roman society and times, similarly, no one can understand Christianity in Africa without adequate knowledge of African culture and religiosity.

40. *New Testament Eschatology*, op. cit., p.190. "Some African Concepts of Christology" in Georg Vicedom, ed., op.cit., p.52.

41. Mbiti, "On the Article of John W. Kinney: A Comment" in *Occasional Bulletin of Missionary Research*, Vol.3, No.2 (1979), p. 68.

42. Mbiti, "Christianity and African Culture," in *Journal of Theology for Southern Africa*, No. 20, (Sept. 1977), pp. 26-40.

43. Western theologians have wrestled with the question of culture and Gospel for sometime. See, for example: H. Niebuhr's classic *Christ and Culture*, (London/NEw York: Faber and Faber, 1952); and Paul Tillich's *Theology of Culture* (New York: Oxford University Press, 1959). Mbiti thinks that the view that Christ

fulfills culture, its transformation not withstanding, is the most profitable for the development of African theology.

CHAPTER THREE

1. "New Testament Eschatology and the Akamba of Kenya," in David Barrett, ed., *African Initiatives in Religion*, (Nairobi: East African Publishing House, 1971), p. 21.

2. Ibid., p. 20.

3. Mbiti, *African Religions and Philosophy*, op. cit., pp.15-16.

4. Mbiti, Ibid., p. 16.

5. *Christian Eschatology in Relation to Evangelization of Tribal Africa*, the Ph.D. dissertation which John Mbiti wrote for Cambridge University in 1963. It was revised for publication by Oxford Press in 1972 under the title, *New Testament Eschatology in an African Background*. All articles on time and eschatology repeat the view developed in his dissertation, in spite of the criticism that the concept has received since its first appearance.

6. Mbiti, *New Testament Eschatology*, op. cit., p. 1.

7. Ibid., p. 57.

8. Mbiti, *African Religions and Philosophy*, op. cit., p. 27. The material meaning refers to material expectations through planning, investments, and new developments. People do not have to be resigned to their given historical situation any more. They can work to change their social, economic and political position for the better.

9. Ibid., p. 17.

10. In order to avoid a misunderstanding that he fears may arise by association made from the English tenses of past, present, and future, Mbiti uses two Swahili words, *Sasa*, to cover present and

future tenses, and *Zamani*, for the past tense.

11. Mbiti, *African Religion and Philosophy*, op. cit., p. 20.

12. Ibid., p. 21.

13. Ibid., p. 22.

14. Ibid., p. 23.

15. Ibid., p. 27.

16. Mbiti, "The Encounter of Christian Faith and African Religion," in *The Christian Century*, Vol. XCVII, No.27 (Aug. 27- Sept. 3, 1980). p. 818.

17. Mbiti, "African Theology," in *Worldview*, Vol. 16, No. 8., (Aug., 1973). p. 38.

18. Mbiti, *African Religions and Philosophy*, op.cit., p.24.

19. Ibid., p. 24.

20. Helmut Thielicke believes that this concept of depth is valuable to understanding mythical thought. Taking his cue from Nicholas Berdyaev,(*The Meaning of History*, 1949), he says that "myth cannot be dispensed with and it is not there just to mystify the past. Myth is there simply because the subject of history is included in it and hence has to feel and unlock the historical." Then he declares, "To plumb the depths of the ages is to plumb the depths of self. For this reason history cannot be known from without but only from within, i.e., by anamnesis of the basis, goal, and meaning of one's own existence." *The Evangelical Faith*, (Edinburgh: T.& T. Clark, 1974), pp.71-72. Even though Thielicke is not speaking of African myths, what he says about the relation of myth to history is applicable to African historical consciousness.

21. *African Religions and Philosophy*, op. cit., p. 23.

22. Ibid., p.24.

23. Ibid., p. 27.

24. Ibid., p. 25.

25. Mbiti uses the term living-dead for persons who are still in the memory of their surviving relatives. Such a person is in the world of spirits, but not in it completely because the living are constantly bringing that person back in their memories. There is some ambivalence about this term because all spirits share in this dual state (at least from our vantage point in history) of being dead and alive at the same time. They are in the past as well as in the present. In areas where people believe in some form of re-incarnation, as in West Africa, people are born again and become present in their own posterity.

26. *African Religions and Philosophy*, op. cit., p. 26.

27. Ibid., p. 26.

28. Ibid., p. 163.

29. *New Testament Eschatology*, op. cit., p. 133.

30. Ibid., p. 139.

31. Ibid., p. 23.

32. See "Hope, Time and Christian Hope", in *Lumen Vitae*, Vol. XXX, No. 1 (1975), pp. 93-104.

33. *New Testament Eschatology*, op. cit., p. 161.

34. Ibid., p. 168.

35. Ibid., p. 143.

36. Ibid., p. 159.

37. Ibid., p. 144.

38. Exodus 3:14; John 8:58.

39. Ibid., p. 156.

CHAPTER FOUR

1. Mbiti, "Harmony, Happiness and Morality in African Religion," in *The Drew Gateway*, Vol. 43, No. 2 (1973) p. 108. See also *African Religions and Philosophy*, op. cit., p. 108.

2. Mbiti, "An African views American Black Theology," in *Worldview*, Vol. 17, No. 8 (Aug. 1974) p. 41. This article has been reproduced in G.Wilmore and J. Cone, eds., *Black Theology: A Documentary History, 1966-79* (Maryknoll, New York: Orbis, 1979). p. 478.

3. Mbiti, "African Theology," in *Worldview*, Vol. 16, No. 8 (Aug., 1973).

4. Mbiti, "Christianity and African Culture," op. cit., p. 31.

5. Mbiti, "Ways and Means of Communicating the Gospel," in C.G. Baeta, ed., *Christianity in Tropical Africa*, (London: Oxford University Press, 1968), p. 329.

6. Mbiti, *African Religions and Philosophy*, op. cit., p. 92.

7. Ibid., p. 16.

8. There are several standard works on myths in Africa. Some of the major ones are, G. Parrinder, *African Mythology*, 1982; H. Baumann, *Schopfung und Urzeit des Menschen im Mythus der Afrikanischen Volker*, 2nd edition, 1964; U. Beier, *The Origins of Life and Death*, 1966; Paul Radin, ed. *African Folktales*, 1953; K. Arnolt, *African Myths and Legends*, 1979.

9. See *Concepts of God in Africa*, op. cit. pp. 45-55, 161-170.

10. The Shilluk and the Bambuti have such myths.

11. The same idea is found among the Lugbara of Tanzania. See John Middleton, *Lugbara Religion*, (Washington, D.C.: Smithsonian Institute Press, 1960), p. 28.

12. The most elaborate myth in this category is that of the Dogon recorded by Marcel Griaule, *Conversations with Ogotemmeli*, (London: Oxford University Press, 1965).

13. Mbiti, *African Religions and Philosophy*, op. cit., p. 95.

14. Ibid., p. 97.

15. Mbiti, "A Change in the African Concept of Man," in Gnana Robinson, ed., *For the Sake of the Gospel*, (Arasaradi, Madurai: T.T.S. Publications, 1980), p. 56.

16. Ibid., p. 99.

17. By asserting this, it does not mean that the reality of God in the present was not talked about. What it means is that God's presence now as not significant enough for itself. What happened in the present was like premium payments for a life policy that only matures upon a persons death. The enjoyment of life in the present was postponed to the future. The present was a time of hardship according to what Jesus said. To be saved is to be assured of entering into heaven and not entering into the fullness of life in the here and now, a life that continues beyond the grave.

18. Ibid., p. 104.

19. Ibid., p. 104.

20. Ibid., p. 108.

21. Ibid., p. 110.

22. Ibid., p. 115.

23. Mbiti, "A Change in the African Concept of Man," op. cit., p. 56.

24. Mbiti, *New Testament Eschatology*, op. cit., p. 94.

25. Some names are given as a remembrance for the day of birth or death of a family member, or some other significant occasion. Naming often takes on cosmic aspects as a testimony to the fact that human beings are related to other cosmic forces.

26. Mbiti, *African Religions and Philosophy*, op. cit., p. 121.

27. Among the Chewas of Malawi, the initiation ceremonies are done by the *Nyau Cult*, a mask society that re-enacts a liturgical dance which recaptures the primeval harmony that existed at the beginning.The masked dancers represent the spirits of the ancestors, and often the ceremony takes place at the cemetery. A more detailed study of this phenomenon is found in M.J. Schoffeleers, *Symbolic and Social Aspects of Spirit Worship among the Mang'anja*, 1968 (a doctoral thesis presented to the University of Oxford). Engelbert Mveng also describes the initiation rites as symbolic of the struggle between life and death in which life triumphs. See *l'Afrique dans l'Eglise Parole d'un Croyant*, (Paris: Editions L'Harmattan, 1985).

28. Ibid., p. 127.

29. This theme has been depicted very effectively in Ngugi wa Thiong'o, *The River Between*,(London: Heinemann, 1965); also in Chinua Achebe, *Things Fall Apart*,(London: Heinemann, 1958).

30. Mbiti, *African Religions and Philosophy*, op. cit., p. 133.

31. This not a reference to casual sex. It refers to responsible relationships which are acknowledged by society as normal for humanity. Sexual rules and attitudes differ from society to society. Mbiti has a book to his credit on this very vital subject, *Love and Marriage in Africa*, (London: Heineman, 1973).

32. Mbiti, *African Religions and Philosophy*, op. cit., p. 142

33. Mbiti, *African Religions and Philosophy*, op. cit., p. 140.

34. Ibid., p. 143.

35. *Love and Marriage in Africa*, op. cit., p. 82.

36. There are some societies in which a mother stops having sexual relationship when her children, male or female, begin to have children of their own. It is believed that the sexual act has mystical powers which may have an adverse effect on the health of the grandchildren. In such societies, sexual taboos are strictly observed.

37. Mbiti, "Harmony, Happiness and Morality in African Religion," in *The Drew Gateway*, Vol. 43. No. 2. (1973). p. 109.

38. Mbiti, *African Religions and Philosophy*, op. cit., p. 149.

39. Iloanusi, op. cit. p. 123.

40. Mbiti, *African Religions and Philosophy*, op. cit., p. 157.

41. Mbiti, *The Prayers of African Religion*, op. cit., p. 14.

42. Mbiti, *African Religions and Philosophy*, op. cit., p. 159.

43. Ibid., p. 163.

44. Mbiti, "Harmony, Happiness and Morality," in *The Drew Gateway*, Vol. 43, No. 2 (1973), p. 110.

45. Psalm 51:4. NIV. The italics are my emphasis.

46. The term "humanity based" is used to emphasize the fact that even though human beings create culture, at the center of that cultural concerns is humanity itself. Culture is an extension of human expression. Culture is for humanity and not humanity for culture.

47. Mbiti, *African Religions and Philosophy*, op. cit., p. 209.

48. Ibid., p. 210.

49. Mbiti, *African Religions and Philosophy*, op. cit., p. 214.

50. Mbiti, "Some Reflections on African Experience of Salvation Today," in S.J. Samartha, ed., *Living Faiths and Ultimate Goals: Salvation and World Religions*, (Maryknoll, New York: Orbis Books, 1976), p. 113.

51. Ibid., p. 110.

52. Mbiti has a more extensive discussion of sin in a French article, "Le Concept Africain du Peche," in *Flambeau*, No.6, (May 1965), pp.104-107. One point he raises is that Africans feel shame and not guilt. He says that it is being caught doing something wrong which seems to be feared and not the fact of doing it. Mbiti does not seem to give any room to the reality of a bad conscience. It is bad conscience that makes people seek to avoid being caught in the action of doing the forbidden. However, it is not primarily a bad conscience towards God, but towards the act and society.

53. Mbiti, "Some Reflections on African Experience of Salvation Today," op. cit., p. 113.

54. Ibid., p. 113.

55. Mbiti, "Man in African Religion," in Isaac James Mowoe and Richard Bjornson, eds., *Africa and the West*, (New York: Greenwood Press, 1986), p. 65.

56. Mbiti, *The Prayers of African Religion*, op. cit., p. 13.

57. Ibid., p. 66.

58. Romans 8:19.

CHAPTER FIVE

1. Mbiti, "On the Article of John Kinney: A Comment," in *Occasional Bulletin*, Overseas Ministries Study Center, Vol. 3, No. 2, (April 1979). p. 68.

2. Ibid., p. 68.

3. *African Religions and Philosophy*, op. cit., p. 216.

4. Ibid., p. 216.

5. Ibid., p. 217.

6. Ibid. p. 216.

7. William Monk, *Dr Livingstone's Cambridge Lectures*, (Cambridge: Deighton, Bell and Co., 1860), p. 168. The lecture was delivered at the University of Cambridge on 4th December, 1857. This appeal resulted in the formation of the Universities Mission to Central Africa. However, of immediate interest is the mention of commerce even before Christianity, pairing them as forces in the civilization of the African heathen. Perhaps, having been in Africa since 1840, he was unaware of the social evils of capitalism, which Karl Marx tried to expose in the 1848 Communist Manifesto. (Emphasis not mine.)

8. Mbiti, ibid. p. 229-241. "The South African Theology of Liberation: Appreciation and Evaluation," in Samuel Amirtham,ed., *A Vision For Man*, (New Delhi: The Christian Literature Society, 1978), p. 356.

9. *Bible and Theology in African Christianity*, op. cit., p. 194.

10. *African Religions and Philosophy*, op. cit., p. 217.

11. Ibid., p. 217.

12. I have in mind here the Shona Uprising of 1896-7 against the

British settlers, the Maji-Maji Rebellion of 1905-7 in Tanganyika against German rule, and the Chilembwe Rising in 1915 in the then Nyasaland (Malawi) against the British administration. Once the Zulu did beat off a British military force sent against them at the battle of Isandhlwana in 1876. Most of these rebellions were religious in character.

13. *African Religions and Philosophy*, op. cit. p. 218.

14. *African Religions and Philosophy*, op. cit., p. 220.

15. Ibid., p. 265.

16. Ibid., p. 219.

17. Ibid., p. 219.

18. Ibid., p. 218.

19. Ibid., pp. 234-35.

20. Ibid., p. 220.

21. Leopold Sedar Senghor, *Prose and Poetry*, (London: Heinemann, 1976), p. 97.

22. Ibid., p. 97.

23. Ibid. p.97.

24. Ibid., p. 97.

25. Quoted in Sylivia Washington Ba *The Concept of Negritude in the Poetry of Leopold Sedar Songhor*, (Princeton, NJ: Princeton University Press, 1973), p. 12.

26. Mbiti, *African Religions and Philosophy*, op. cit., p. 268.

27. Ibid., p. 269.

28. Ibid., p. 270.

29. According to Paul, Jesus has broken out of the confines of human standards thereby necessitating a paradigm shift in the way humanity is viewed, in that, "when anyone is joined to Christ, he is a new being; the old is gone, the new has come." 2 Cor. 5:16, 17.(Goodnews Bible) Jesus transcends cultural identities.

30. Mbiti, *Human Development Through Credit Unions*, op. cit., p. 79.

31. Philippians 2: 12,13. NIV. Paradoxically the historical outworking of salvation involves taking responsibility for it, not autonomously but theonomously. Salvation, as a historical event, implies material development also besides a spiritual relationship.

32. See James Cone, *A Black Theology of Liberation*, second Edition, (Maryknoll, New York: Orbis Books, 1986), especially chapters four and six. Also his *Black Theology and Black Power*, (Minneapolis, Minnesota: Seabury Press, 1969). Gayraud Wilmore, *Black Religion and Black Radicalism*, (Maryknoll, New York: Orbis Books, 1973). Albert Cleage, *The Black Messiah*, (New York: Sheed and Ward, 1968). Papers from the conference on "The Black Revolution: Is there a Black Theology?" which took place in 1968. The papers were printed in *The Journal of Religious Thought*, Vol. XXVI, No. 2, 1969. At this conference there were dissenting voices to the use of the concept. (See articles by Frank Wilson, Richard McKinney, and Leon Wright.) The major reason was that they wanted to emphasize universality and inclusivity rather than particularity and exclusivity which advocates of the concept of blackness championed. There are others who also have expressed their misgivings about the use of the term blackness in theology, for instance, Robert Duke, "Black theology and the Experience of Blackness" in *The Journal of Religious Thought*, Vol. XXIX, No. 1. 1972. Tom Skinner, *How Black is the Gospel?* (Philadelphia: Lippincott, 1970). Perhaps James Cone represents the most radical position presented yet on the concept of Blackness. John Mbiti was quite aware of some of this literature

when he wrote his assessment having spent a year teaching at Union Theological Seminary with James Cone in 1972-3.

33. Mbiti, "An African views American Black Theology," in *Worldview*, op. cit. p. 42.

34. Mbiti may not have been aware of the US legal definition of a black person as anyone who had a fraction of "black" blood. Such a definition can only serve to maintain "purity" of the caucasian race. The issue in the USA was not color variation, but one of racial defilement.

35. Mbiti, "An African Views American Black Theology," in *Worldview*, op. cit., p. 41.

36. John 8:31, NRSV.

37. Mbiti, "The South African Theology of Liberation: Appreciation and Evaluation," op. cit., 1978.

38. Ibid., p. 358.

39. Ibid., p. 356.

40. This position is in line with what the writer to the Ephesians says about the work of Christ: "For he is our peace; in his flesh he has made both groups into one and has broken down the dividing wall, that is, the hostility between us." 2: 14, NRSV.

41. It is a chapter contribution in Gnana Robinson, ed., *For the Sake of the Gospel*, op. cit., pp. 54-63.

42. Ibid., p. 59.

43. Ibid., pp. 60-61.

44. *African Religions and Philosophy*, op. cit., p. 27.

45. Mbiti, *New Testament Eschatology*, op. cit., p. 168.

46. Ibid., p. 169.

47. Mbiti, *African Religions and Philosophy*, op. cit., p. 277.

CHAPTER SIX

1. Perhaps the most vehement and sustained criticism has come from two people who speak from radically different perspectives and yet seem to support each other in their critique of Mbiti. The two are the late Okot p'Bitek in *Western Scholarship and the Study of African Religion*, (Nairobi: East African Publishing House, 1970?), and Byang Kato in *Theological Pitfalls in Africa*, (Kisumu: Evangel Publishing House, 1975). p'Bitek accused Mbiti, among others, of dressing African deities in hellenistic robes while Kato accused Mbiti of advocating universalism and abetting syncretism.

2. Kwesi Dickson, *Aspects of Religion and Life in Africa*, (Accra: Ghana Academy of Arts and Science, 1977), p. 10.

3. Ibid., p. 10.

4. Benjamin Ray, "Recent Studies of African Religions" in *History of Religions*, Vol. 12, Number 1, (Aug. 1972), pp.75-89.

5. Lugano Sankey, "African Concept of Time" in *African Theological Journal*, Makumira Lutheran Theological College, Tanzania, No.2, (Feb. 1969), pp.95-101.

6. John Parratt, "Time in Traditional African Thought," in *Religion*, Vol. 7, Part Two, (Autumn) 1977. pp. 117-126.

7. Francis Gillies, "The Bantu Concept of Time" in *Religion*, (London: Routledge and Kegan Paul, 1980), pp.16-30.

8. Benjamin Ray, *History of Religions*, op.cit., pp.75-89.

9. E. Ruch, "Philosophy of African History," in *African Studies*, Vol. 32. No. 2 (1972), p.122.

10. John Parratt, "Time in Traditional African Thought," op. cit. pp. 117-126.

11. Benjamin Ray, *African Religions*, (Englewood Cliffs, NJ: Prentice-Hall, inc., 1976), p. 41.

12. B. W. Burleson, *John Mbiti*, Doctor of Philosophy Dissertation presented to the faculty of Baylor University, Texas, U.S.A. 1986, p. 123.

13. Ibid., p. 127.

14. Ibid., p. 135.

15. Ibid., p. 138.

16. Mbiti does not subscribe to this cyclic view, even though Burleson thinks he does. Mbiti simply reverses the western linear view. However, notwithstanding the aforesaid, Mbiti is uncritical of the norms or models of time that he appropriates from the western cultures.

17. E. Ruch, "Philosophy of African History," in *African Studies*, Vol. 32, No. 2, 1973. pp. 113-126.

18. Ironically, he thus goes against his own principle that "man is not a slave to time." See *African Religions and Philosophy*, op. cit., p. 19.

19. Ibid., p. 23.

20. We legitimately speak of African civilization to mean the humanization process as it is expressed in and through social, cultural, economic, political, and technological arrangements leading to a quality of life spiritually and materially. For material and cultural progress, which Europe denied Africa in the past, recent revisions of African history have documented abundant evidence. See the multi-volume *General History of Africa* (UNESCO 1981, 1990), especially volumes I and II, edited by J.

Ki-Zerbo and G. Mokhtar respectively.

21. The fact that many Africanist scholars are of the view that there is definitely a future dimension of time contrary to Mbiti's claims, and if the norm for determining time is taken from African experience and not from Christian eschatology and western linear view of time, the assertions that follow would be borne out from the experiences of the many peoples in Malawi and I am sure in Kenya among the Akamba as well. Richard Gehman in *Doing African Christian Theology*, Nairobi: Evangel Publishing House, 1987, pp. 66-71, has among other things looked at the grammar of Kikamba in relation to the future tense, claims that Mbiti's position is not tenable. However, given the New Testament eschatological view of time as the standard used to determine African view of time, then Mbiti is right to say that such a future does not exist in African conception.

22. The Ndali people say, *Akabalilo kabuka*, meaning time is gone. So also the Tumbuka and the Chewa peoples of Malawi. It is possible to speak of the passage of time without consciously thinking of a clock. Similarly, Africans speak of the passage of time without consciously recalling the movement of the sun, or seasons by which they usually reckon time's movement. The point is that it is not simply what humans do that determines time, but also the very fact of their existence.

23. Mbiti, *New Testament Eschatology in an African Background*, op. cit., p. 24.

24. Mbiti, *African Religions and Philosophy*, op. cit., p. 212.

25. Thomas Cullen Young develops this idea of a Good Village in his book *African Ways and Wisdom*, (London: United Society for Christian literature, 1937). The idea came to him from the Tumbuka people of Northern Malawi where the term *Muzi uweme* is used. The words do not refer to the external looks of the village, its gardens, architecture, setting, and lay-out, but rather to the character of the people who live in it. When he enquired about

the meaning of the statement, he was told: "A good village is where the headman and the elders are respected by all; and where they too have regard for all, even for children. It is a good village where the young respect parents and where no one tries to harm another. If there is even one person who belittles another person or works harm, then the village is spoiled." p. 12

26. Engelbert Mveng, *l'Afrique dans l'Église...* op. cit., p.17.

27. "...c'est l'homme divisé qui devise le monde." My translation which was checked by Rev. Vangu Lusakweno of Zaire. It is quoted by Oscar Bimwenyi-Kweshi, *Discours Théologique Négro-Africain*, (Paris: Presence Africaine, 1981), p. 595.

28. Mbiti, *African Religions and Philosophy*, op. cit., p. 214.

29. Among the Bandali people found on both sides of the border between Tanzania and Malawi, swearing is done either in the name of a dead parent, grandparent, or all the dead collectively, current and long forgotten. The dead continue to live along with the living, but on a different existential level.

30. E. Ruch, "Philosophy of African history," op. cit., p. 119.

31. Mbiti, *African Religions and Philosophy*, op. cit., p. 98.

32. Ibid., p. 99.

33. Engelbert Mveng, *l'Afrique dans l'Église...* op. cit. p. 10ff.

34. O.A.Iloanusi, *Myths of the Creation of Man and the Origin of Death in Africa: A Study in Igbo Traditional Culture and Other African Cultures*, (Frankfurt am Main: Peter Lang, 1984), p. 224.

35. Ibid., p. 226. Salvation from death is sought after when one has not attained to old age, a point at which death is accepted as welcome and natural. It is here that one looks toward what Iloanusi refers to as eschatological salvation. This is life beyond the grave.

36. Mbiti, *New Testament Eschatology*, op. cit., p. 139.

37. Oscar Bimwenyi-Kweshi, *Discours Théologique Négro-Africain*, op. cit. pp. 587-593.

38. Engelbert Mveng, *l'Afrique dans l'Église...* op. cit. pp. 10-12.

39. Iloanusi, op.cit., p. 123.

40. Mbiti, *Poems of Nature and Faith*, (Nairobi: East African Publishing House, 1969). See the following poems: "Man's Lost Immortality;" "Men without Death;" "Beyond these Phenomena."

41. Engelbert Mveng has a very appropriate term that describes this experience in an essay "Third world Theology- What Theology? What third World?: Evaluation by an african Delegate." He calls it "anthropological poverty." He states, "It consists in despoiling human beings not only of what they have, but of everything that constitutes their being and essence--their identity, history, ethnic roots, language, culture, faith, creativity, dignity, pride, ambitions, right to speak..." See Virginia Fabella and Sergio Torres, eds., *The Irruption of the Third World: Challenge to Theology*, (Maryknoll, New York: Orbis Books, 1983), p. 220.

42. Being a Kenyan in whose country Mau-Mau was fought due to racist policies of the colonial regime, Mbiti needs not to be reminded of this sad history. However, that history is part of the collective experience of black people. Since racism becomes a worldview in its own right, it determines perception on most fronts and the socializing process in the dominant culture. Isolated racist incidents are symptomatic of an underlying racist worldview.

43. Alexander Hetherwick, *The Gospel and the African*, (Edinburgh: T. & T. Clark, 1932), p. 172.

44. Until after independence, African history was the history of Euro-American white people in Africa. Since independence African history is being rewritten with the Africans as the subjects

of history and other people as incidental to it.

45. In the Western understanding of humanity material progress has been one of the indexes used to define humanity. Technological superiority has meant superior humanity and thus a superior race. With western culture predominating at present, Africa will be judged by those standards unless the people of Africa refuse to be defined by others. It will need concerted voice from all aspects of life to do this. African Theology is doing its part.

46. Galatians 3:28.

47. cf. John 10:10. To be relevant to Malawian thought pattern, this text could also be rendered thus: "I came that they may be human and have *humanness* in its true sense." To Malawians the word humanity has the connotations of a quality of life (*Moyo*).

48. In John 3: 16 and Luke 4:16ff, God's love as inclusive of black humanity is very clear.

49. In John 10:10 Jesus describes his mission in terms of abundance of life, while in Matt. 5:48, he describes the human goal as perfection.

50. See Okot p'Bitek, *Western Scholarship and the Study of African Religion*. Kampala, Uganda: East African Literature Bureau, 1971.

51. In an essay "Where are we in African Theology" in Kofi Appiah-Kubi and Sergio Torres, *African Theology en Route*. Maryknoll, NY: Orbis Books, 1979; Setiloane castigates Mbiti for "...much too simplistically drawing up similarities between African traditional understanding and the Christian faith." p. 62.

52. Mbiti, *African Religions and Philosophy*, op. cit., p. 24.

53. In a conversation with Mbiti, he explained that when one does pioneering work one uses what is current in terminology in order

53. In a conversation with Mbiti, he explained that when one does pioneering work one uses what is current in terminology in order to engage in the debate effectively.

54. S.J. Samartha, ed. *Living Faiths and Ultimate Goals*, (Geneva: WCC, 1974), pp. 108-119.

55. Ibid., p. 110.

56. Patrick Kalilombe argues for the salvific value of African traditional religions in "The Salvific Value of African Religions" *African Ecclessiatical Review*, Vol.21, No.3, (1979). Using God's cosmic covenant as his point of departure, he asserts, "...as long as these religions were the serious searchings of our culture for deity, they are to be respected as the normal divinely-given means of salvation, put by God in his will for the salvation of all the peoples," p.156. Samuel Kibicho argues for the presence of salvation in traditional religions of the Kikuyu. See "The Continuity of the African Conception of God into and through Christianity; a Kikuyu Case-study," in E. Fashole-Luke and others, eds., *Christianity in Independent Africa*, Rex Collings, (London: 1978), pp.370-388.

57. Mbiti, *Concepts of God in Africa*,(London: S.P.C.K., 1970), p. 247.

58. "Hope, Time and Christian Hope," in *Lumen Vitae*, No. 1, Vol. XXX(1975), p. 103.

59. Matthew 5:13,14.

60. "Some African Concepts of Christology," op. cit., p. 56.

61. Mbiti, "An African views American Black Theology," in Wilmore and Cone, eds., *Black Theology: A Documentary History, 1966-1979*, (Maryknoll, New York: Orbis Books, 1979), p. 478.

62. Jesus revealed this reality when he told the Jews: "Before Abraham was, I am." John 8:58, RSV. In this saying Jesus was

claiming the character of God as revealed to Moses when he was being sent to back to Egypt.

CHAPTER SEVEN

1. Gen. 1:26-27.

2. In Malawi a distinction is made between *munthu*, the human person and *chinthu*, (a thing or beast). These are characteristically opposites. Human persons who show no human integrity in their behavior redefine themselves by their very action as *chinthu*. Even worse, they can become *chinthu cha waka* (Tumbuka), meaning a valueless thing.

3. Oscar Bimwenyi-Kweshi, *Discours Théologique Négro-Africain: Problème des Fondements.*, op. cit. p. 586.

4. Ibid., p. 587.

5. A Malawian song states that hatred is to differ in speech because words have been corrupted. Therefore, a good word always contributes to the up building of a Good Community.

6. E. K. Twesigye, *The Global Human Problem: Ignorance, Hate, Injustice and Violence*, (New York: Peter Lang, 1989), p.75.

7. Ephesians 2:14-18.

8. Ephesians 4:13.

9. Luke 2:52. It is important to distinguish wisdom from knowledge. Wisdom is the ability to use knowledge to choose the right means for the right ends for the benefit of oneself and the community. The Bible links wisdom with reverence for God. Wisdom takes into account righteousness and reverence for life. Knowledge is neutral. It can be for good or evil ends, while wisdom at all times seeks right ends.

10. Unfaithfulness results when idols of power, greed, racism,

sexism, cultural imperialism and even theology take the place of God in determining human relationships.

11. In an article, "A Philosophy of the Human Person for Contemporary Theology," Augustine Shutte defines the human person in terms of spirituality understood as "possessing the capacity for self-enactment of the radical kind that shows itself in distinctively human self-consciousness and self-determination." He attempts to overcome the Thomistic duality of spirituality and materiality by define them in term of each other. He states that we human persons realize our [spiritual] power of self-enactment in a radical [material] dependence on other persons. See *Journal of Theology For Southern Africa*, No. 14, (Dec. 1982), pp.74-75.

12. Jean-Marc Ela, *African Cry*, (Maryknoll, New York: Orbis Books, 1986), p. 87.

13. Ibid., p. 88.

14. 2 Cor. 5: 14-16.

15. I would rather have "other" in place of "second" to avoid the impression of a hierarchical structure instead of complementarity of gender in the definition of our humanity.

16. E. Mveng, "African Liberation Theology." in L. Boff and V. Elizondo, eds., *Theologies of the Third World: Convergences and Differences*, (Edinburgh: T and T Clark Ltd., 1988), p. 32.

17. Mercy Oduyoye, *Hearing and Knowing*, op. cit., especially p. 35ff.

18. Matt. 19:8.

19. Paul made concession when he had Timothy circumcised (Acts 16:1-5), and had the hair shaven of the gentile Christians who were visiting Jerusalem with him (Acts 21: 17-26). In his first letter to the Corinthians, he makes a number of concession and guidelines.

20. Ela, *African Cry*, op. cit., p. 86.

21. Mark 2:27.

22. Mbiti, *African Religions and Philosophy*, op. cit., p. 277.

Bibliography

PRIMARY WORKS

A. BOOKS

Mbiti, John S. *Mutunga na Ngewa Yake*. Nairobi: East African Literature Bureau, 1954.

_____. *English-Kamba Vocabulary*. Nairobi: East African Literature Bureau, 1959.

_____. *Akamba Stories*. London: Oxford University Press, 1966.

_____. *The People of God*. Geneva: World Student Christian Federation, 1962.

_____. *African Religions and Philosophy*. London: Heinemann, 1969.

_____. *Poems of Nature and Faith*. Nairobi: East African Publishing House, 1969. Publishing House, 1969.

_____. *Concepts of God in Africa*. London: S.P.C.K., 1970.

_____. *The Crisis of Mission in Africa*. Mukono, Uganda: Church Press, 1971.

_____. *New Testament Eschatology in an African Background*. London: Oxford University Press, 1972.

_____. *Love and Marriage in Africa*. London: Heinemann, 1973.

_____. *The Voice of Nine Bible Trees*. Kampala: Church of Uganda Press, 1973.

_____. *An Introduction to African Religion*. London: Heinemann, 1975.

_____. *The Prayers of African Religion*. Maryknoll, New York: Orbis Books, 1975.

_____. ed., *Confessing Christ in Different Cultures*. Bossey, Switzerland: World Council of Churches, 1977.

_____. ed., *African and Asian Contribution to Contemporary Theology*. Bossey, Switzerland: World Council of Churches, 1977.

_____. ed., *Christian and Jewish Dialogue on Man*. Bossey, Switzerland: World Council of Churches, 1978.

_____. *Indigenous Theology and the Universal Church*. Bossey, Switzerland: World Council of Churches, 1979.

_____. *Bible and Theology in African Christianity*. Nairobi: Oxford University Press, 1986.

B. *ARTICLES BY JOHN MBITI*

Mbiti, John S. "African Christians and the Jewish Religion." *Christian Attitudes on Jews and Judaism*, 56 (Oct. 1977):1-4.

_____. "African Christians and Jewish Religious Heritage." *Christian-Jewish Relations in Ecumenical Perspective*, Franz von Hammerstein, ed., Geneva: World Council of Churches, 1978: 13-19.

_____. "African Concept of Human Relations." in *Ministry*, 9,

(Oct. 1969): 158-62.

_____. "African Concept of Time, History and Death." *in Afrika: German Review of Political, Economic and Cultural Affairs in Africa and Madagascar* 8 (1967): 33-38.

_____. "African Indigenous Culture in relation to Evangelism and Church Development." in *The Gospel and Frontier Peoples*, edited by R. Pierce Beaver. Pasadena, California: William Carey Library, 1973: 79-95.

_____. "African Names of God." in *Orita*, 6, (June 1972): 3-14.

_____. "African Religion," in *The Study of Spirituality*, edited by Cheslyn Jones and others. New York: Oxford university Press, 1986: 513-516.

_____. "African Religion and its Contribution to World Order." in *Spirituality and World Order*, edited by Patricia Mische, East Orange, NJ: Global Education Associates, 1982:27-31.

_____. "African Students in East Germany." in *Rock*, 76, (March 1964): 2.

_____. "African Theology," in *Worldview*, Vol. 16, No. 8, (Aug. 1973): 33-39.

_____. "African Traditional Medicine and its Relevance for Christian Work." in *So Sende Ich Euch: Festschrift fur Dr. Martin Porksen*, edited by Otto van Waack, J. Freytag, and G. Hoffmann. Stuttgart: Evangel, Missionverlag, 1973: 310-18.

_____. "An African Views American Black Theology." in *Worldview* 17, (Aug. 1974): 41-44.

_____. "Apport Africain a l'eglise?" *Flambeau* 7, (Aug. 1965): 165-69.

_____. "The Biblical Basis for Present Trends in African Theology." *African Theological Journal* 7, (1978): 72-85. Also in *African Theology en Route*, edited by Kofi Appiah-Kubi and Sergio Torres. Maryknoll, New York: Orbis Books, 1979.

_____. "Blessed are those who mourn, for they shall be comforted." in ...*And Yet Be Happy: The Beatitudes Revisited*, edited by Emido Campi. Geneva: World Students Christian Federation, 1981: 29-32.

_____. "Bossey: A Living Experience." *One World* 11, (Nov. 1975): 20.

_____. ""Cattle are born with Ears, Their Horns Grow later." Towards an Appreciation of Oral Theology." in *African Theological Journal* 8, No.1, (1979): 15-25.

_____. "A Change of the African Concept of Man Through Christian Influence," in *For the Sake of the Gospel*, edited by Gnana Robinson. Madurai, India: T.T.S. Publications, 1980.

_____. "The Christian Faith in Africa." *Ecumenical News*, 7, (July 1977): 6-9.

_____. "Christianity and African Culture," in *Journal of Theology for Southern Africa*, No. 20, (Sept. 1977): 26-40.

_____. "Christianity and African Religion." in *Facing the New Challenges*, edited by Michael Cassidy and Luc Verlinden. Kisumu, Kenya: Evangel Publishing House, 1978: 308-13.

_____. "Christianity and African Religious Heritage." in *The*

Virginia Seminary Journal, 26, (Jan. 1974): 10-16.

_____. "Christianity and Traditional Religions in Africa," in *International review of Mission* 59, (1970): 430-440.

_____. "Christianity is Replacing Native Religions in Africa." *Presence Africaine* 2, (Aug-Nov. 1958): 129-53.

_____. "Church and State: A Neglected Element of Christianity in Contemporary Africa." *Africa Theological Journal* 5, (Dec. 1972): 31-42.

_____. "The Church in Africa Today." in *Christian Living Today*, edited by J. Lucker and G. McKenna. London: Geoffrey Chapman. 1974: C1-C3.

_____. "The Church of Uganda, Rwanda and Burundu in the 1970's." *Pan-Anglican: Review of the Worldwide Episcopal Church*, 15, (1970): 77-82.

_____. "The Concept of God in Jewish and African Traditions." in *Christian-Jewish Relations in Ecumenical Perspectives*, edited by Franz von Hammerstein. Geneva: World Council of Churches, 1978.

_____. "The Concept of Time." in *Student Manual: African Worldview*, edited by H. Olela and C. Snowden. Washington, DC: Institute of Services of Education, 1971: 167-76.

_____. "Diversity, Divisions and Denominationalism." in *Kenya Churches Handbook*, edited by David Barrett et al. Kisumu, Kenya: Evangel Publishing House, 1973.

_____. "Division or Unity,"in *One World*, (Feb. 1975): 12-13.

_____. "The Encounter of Christian Faith and African

Religion," in *The Christian Century*, (Aug. 27-Sept. 1980): 817-820.

_____. "Eschatology," in *Biblical Revelation and African Beliefs*, edited by Kwesi Dickson and Paul Ellingworth, Maryknoll, New York: Orbis Books, 1969.

_____. "Faith Hope and Love in the African Independent Church Movement." *Study Encounter* 10, (Oct. 1974): 1-19.

_____. "Focus on: the Gospel and Culture——a Living Issue." *Reformed Press Service*, 175 (October 1979): 6-7.

_____. "The Forest Has Ears." *Peace, Happiness and Prosperity*, 7 (July 1976): 17-26.

_____. "The Future of Christianity in Africa (1970-2000)." *Communio Viatorum:Theological Quarterly* 13 (1970): 19-38.

_____. "The Future of Christianity in Africa." *Cross Currents*, 28 (Winter 1978-79): 387-94.

_____. "God, Dreams and African Militancy," in *Religion in a Pluralistic Society*, edited by John S. Pobee. Leiden: E.J. Brill, 1076: 38-47.

_____. "Gospel, Faith and Culture." *Image: Christ and Art in Asia* 3 (March 1980): 2.

_____. "The Gospel in African Cultural Context." in *Towards Theology in an Australian Context*, edited by Victor C. Hayes. Bedford Park, South Australia: Australian Association for the Study of Religions Publications, Stuart College of Advanced Education, 1979: 18-26.

_____. "The Growing Respectability of African Traditional

Religion." *Lutheran World,* 19 (1972): 54-58.

_____. "Harmony, Happiness and Morality in African Religion," in *The Drew Gateway,* 43, No. 2, (1973): 108-115.

_____. "He who has not travelled thinks that his mother is the best cook in the world." In *Indigenous Theology and the Universal Church,* edited by John Mbiti. Bossey, Switzerland: Ecumenical Institute, 1979.

_____. " Hope, Time and Christian Hope," in *Lumen Vitae,* Vol.XXX, No. 1, (1975): 93-104.

_____. "How deep is Christianity in East Africa." *Rock,* 45 (Aug. 1961): 1.

_____. "Is God a Hindrance or A Basis for Intellectual Development?" in *Presence,* vol. IV, No.1, (1970) 26-32.

_____. "Is Science Running Ahead of Religion?" *Panoramic Makerere* (Oct. 1970): 15-16.

_____. "The Kamba of Central Kenya:...Family Planning; Taboo Regarding Sex, Birth and Children; Sex Education and (Kikamba) Vocabulary." in *Cultural Source Materials for Population Planning in East Afric,* edited by Angela Molnos. Nairobi: East African Publishing House, 1973: 126-33.

_____. "The Kamba of Central Kenya: Religious Beliefs and Fertility; Traditional Naming Customs; Female Fertility and Proper Woman; Male sex, life and fertility; Children's symbolic significance and value." In *Beliefs and Practices* edited by Angela Molnos. Nairobi: East African Publishing House, 1973: 97-105.

_____. "La Concept Africain du Péche," in *Flambeau,* No. 6,

(1965): 104-107.

_____. "Man: Potential and Devoted." *Peace, Happiness and Prosperity* (Jan. 1973): 65-68.

_____. "Mission Outreach in African Theology." In *Christian Theology and Strategy for Mission*, edited by Rebecca Schmutz. Geneva: Lutheran World Federation, 1980: 172-98.

_____. "Moratorium Opposed." *Target* 134a (21 July, 1974):4.

_____. "New Testament Eschatology and The Akamba of Kenya," in *African Initiatives in Religion*, edited by David Barrett. Nairobi: East African Publishing House, 1971: 17-30.

_____. "New Testament Eschatology in an African Back ground." *Readings in Dynamic Indigeneity*, edited by Charles H. Kraft and Tom N. Wisley. Pasadena, California: William Carey Library, 1979: 455-64.

_____. "On the Article of John W. Kinney: A Comment," in *Occasional Bulletin of Missionary Research*, Vol. 3, No. 2, (1979): 69.

_____. "[Our Savior] as an African Experience," in *Christ and Spirit in the New Testament*, edited by Barnabbas. Lindars and S. S. Smalley, London: Cambridge University Press, 1973: 397-414.

_____. "Our Stand Towards African Traditional Religion." *Write* 1 (1973): 9-17.

_____. "Some African Concepts of Christology," in *Christ and the Younger Churches*, edited by Georg Vicedom. London: S.P.C.K., 1972. pp. 51-62.

_____. "Some Aspects of African Religion." In *Essays on the African Arts and Humanities*, edited by Rand Bishop, N.p., 1973.

_____. "Some Current Concerns of African Theology," in *Expository Times*, Vol. LXXXVII, No. 6. (1976): 164-168. Also in *African and Asian Contributions to Contemporary Theology: Report*, edited by John Mbiti. Bossey, Switzerland: Ecumenical Institute of WCC, 1976. pp. 6-17.

_____. "Some Reflection on African Experience of Salvation Today," *Living Faiths and Ultimate Goals: Salvation and World Religions*, edited by Stanley J. Samartha. Maryknoll, New York: Orbis Books, 1975.pp. 108-119.

_____. "The South African Theology of Liberation: Appreciation and Evaluation," in *A Vision for Man*, edited by Samuel Amirtham. Madras: Christian Literature Society, 1978. pp. 348-358.

_____. "Some Theological and Related Questions About "Human Development"" in Second *World Conference on Human Development Through Credit Unions*. Bossey, Switzerland: World Council of credit Unions, 1975. pp. 77-80. (Mimeographed)

_____. " Theological Impotence and the Universality of the Church," in *Mission Trends No.3: Third World Theologies*, edited by G. Anderson and T. Stransky. New York: Paulist Press, 1976. pp. 6-18.

_____."Traditional African Thinking (1): Religion." *Pro Veritate*, 11 (June 1972): 3.

_____."Traditional African Thinking (2): The Essence of Things." *Pro Veritate*, 11 (July 1972): 14.

_____. " Traditional African Thinking (3): Concept of Time."
Pro Veritate, 11 (Aug. 1972): 11.

_____. "Traditional African Thinking (4): Concept of
Chronology." *Pro Veritate*, 11 (Sept. 1972): 11.

_____. "Traditional African Thinking (5): Concept of History."
Pro Veritate, 11 (Nov. 1972): 23.

_____. "Traditional Religions in Africa." In *Historical Atlas of
the Religions of the World*, edited by Ismail al-faruqi and
D.E. Sopher. New York: Macmillan Publishing Co., Inc.,
1975. pp. 61-68.

_____. "The Ways and Means of Communicating the Gospel."
In *Christianity in Tropical Africa*, Edited by C.G. Baeta.
London: Oxford University Press, 1968. pp. 329-50.

_____. "What God is Saying...through the African Independent
Churches to the Western Churches." *Risk* 7 (1971):56-58.

_____. "Why Christian Mission Today?" *New World Outlook*,
33 (June 1973): 19-20.

_____. "Worship." in *Presence*, Vol.V, No. 3, 1972. pp.23-25.

C. REVIEWS BY JOHN MBITI
Mbiti, John S. Review of Alyward Shorter, *African Christian
Theology: Adaptation or Incarnation*, in *International Review
of Mission*, 67, (April 1978): 223-24.

_____. Review of Newell S. Booth, Jr. ed., *African Religions: A
Symposium*, in *International Review of Mission*, 68, (July
1978): 319-20.

_____. Review of Benjamin Ray *African Religions: Symbols,*

Ritual, and Community, in *Worldview,* (June 1976): 55-56.

_____. Review of *African Tradition and the Christian God,* by Charles Nyamiti. *International Bulletin of Missionary Research,* 5 (1981): 41-42.

_____. Review of *Christianity in Independent Africa,* edited by Edward Fashole-Luke et al. in *International Review of Missions* 70 (April 1981): 76-78.

_____. Review of *The New Religions of Africa,* edited by Bennetta Jule-Rosette in *International Review of Missions* 70 (April 1981): 78-79.

D. *UNPUBLISHED SOURCES BY MBITI*

Mbiti, John S. "African Christianity in the Context of Transition, Change and Modernization." A lecture given at the Hebrew University, Jerusalem, June 1977.

_____. "African Identity in Religion and Literature." A lecture given at Das Institut fur Afrikanistik der Universtat zu Koln, West Germany, 27 April 1978.

_____. "A Bird Does Not Build with Other Birds' Feathers." An Address given at Makerere University, Kampala, Uganda, January 1972.

_____. "Christian Eschatology in Relation to Evangelization of Tribal Africa." Ph. D. dissertation, Cambridge University, 1963.

_____. "Christianity Tilts to the South." The Ransden University Sermon at the Great St. Mary's Church, University of Cambridge, England, 29 May 1977.

_____. "Comments on the Issue of Spirit Possession and the Church." A lecture given in Arusha, Tanzania, July 1981.

_____. "Contextual Theology, an African Perspective." A lecture given at the Ecumenical Institute of the World Council of Churches, Bossey, Switzerland, 10 August 1985.

_____. "Death as Focus of Fear, Faith and Future." A lecture given at the Ecumenical Institute, Bossey, Switzerland, August 1975.

_____. "From Chalcedon October 451 to Bossey 1976: Towards an Ecumenical Christology." An address given to the Graduate School of Ecumenical Studies at the Ecumenical Institute, Bossey, Switzerland, 14 October 1976.

_____. "Glory, Glory to the Lamb: One Form of Confessing Christ in Africa." Lecture given at the Ecumenical Institute, Bossey, 1974.

_____. "Indigenous Theology and the Universal Church." A lecture given to Evangelisches Missionswerk im Bereich der Bundersrepublik Deutschland und Berlin West e.v. ——Geschattsstelle, Bossey, Switzerland, 28 September 1978.

_____. "Jesus Christ Frees and Unites." An address to the Graduate School of the Ecumenical Institute, Bossey, Switzerland, 15 August 1974.

_____. "Mission Outreach in African Theology." A paper given in preparation For the All-Africa Lutheran Conference on Christian Theology and Strategy for Mission in the African Context, Monrovia, Liberia, July 1979.

_____. "Religious Values." A paper given at the Conference on "The Search for Absolute Values: Harmony among the Sciences," Washington, 26 November 1976.

_____. "The Role of the African Church in the Ecumenical Movement." A lecture given at the Ecumenical Institute, Bossey, Switzerland, 27 May 1978.

_____. "Seeking Community: The Common Search of People of Various Faiths, Cultures and Ideologies." A lecture given at the Ecumenical Institute, Bossey, n.d.

_____. "Some Aspects of African Religion in Respect to World Order." A lecture given to the Lindisfarne Association, New York, 30 November 1978.

_____. "Some Parallels Between Jewish and African Religious Life." A paper presented at the Consultation on Church and Jewish People, Jerusalem, June 1977.

_____. "Who do you say that I am?" A lecture given to the Graduate School of the Ecumenical Institute, Bossey, 14 October 1976.

_____. "Why did God make me (man)?: An African Reply." A lecture given at the Ecumenical Institute, Bossey, March 1977.

_____. "'Your Kingdom Come': World Conference on Mission and Evangelism." A lecture given at the Ecumenical Institute, Bossey, July 1979.

Interviews

Mbiti, John S. Burgdorf, Switzerland. Interview, 4-9th June 1989.

Secondary Sources

A. BOOKS

Abraham, W.E. *The Mind of Africa.* Chicago: The University of

Chicago Press, 1962.

Adeyemo, Tokunboh. *Salvation in African Tradition*. Kisumu, Kenya: Evangel Publishing House, 1979.

Alves, Rubem. *The Theology of Human Hope*. St. Meinrad, Indiana: Abbey Press, 1972.

Anderson, Gerald and Stransky, Thomas, eds. *Mission Trends No.1*. New York and Grand Rapids: Paulist Press and William Eerdmans Publishing Co., 1981.

_____. *Mission Trends No. 3: Third World Theologies*, 1976.

_____. *Mission Trends No. 4: Liberation theologies*, 1979.

_____. *Mission Trends No. 5: Faith Meets Faith*, 1981.

Anderson, Ray. *On Being Human*. Grand Rapids: W.B. Eerdmans Publishing Company, 1982.

Appiah-Kubi, Kofi; and Torres, Sergio, eds., *African Theology en Route*. Maryknoll, New York: Orbis Books, 1979.

Asante, Molefi and Asante, Kariam. *African Culture: The Rhythms of Unity*: Trenton, New Jersey: Africa World Press, 1990.

Asante, Molefi. *Afrocentricity*. revised edition. Trenton, New Jersey: Africa World Press, 1988.

Beaver, R. Pierce, ed. *The Gospel and Frontier Cultures*. Pasadena, California: William Carey Library, 1973.

Becken, Hans-Jurgen. ed. *Relevant Theology for Africa*. Natal: Lutheran Publishing House, 1973.

Biko, Steve. *I Write What I Like*, London: Heinemann Educational Books, 1979.

Bimwenye-Kweshi, Oscar. *Discours Théologique Négro-Africaine*. Paris: Présence Africaine, 1981.

Boahen, A. Adu. *General History of Africa: Africa Under Colonial Domination 1880-1935*, Vol. VII, Abridged edition. California: James Carey (UNESCO), 1985.

Boesak, Allan. *Farewell to Innocence: A Socio-Ethical Study on Black Theology and Power*. Maryknoll, New York: Orbis Books, 1976.

_____. *Black and Reformed: Apartheid, Liberation and the Calvinist Tradition*. Maryknoll, New York: Orbis Books, 1984.

Boff, Leonardo and Virgil Elizondo. *Theologies of the Third World: Convergences and Differences*. Edinburgh: T and T Clark, 1988.

Boulaga, F. Eboussi. *Christianity Without Fetishes: An African Critique and Recapture of Christianity*. Maryknoll, New York: Orbis Books, 1981.

Bozeman, Adda, B. *Conflict in Africa: Concepts and Realities*. Princeton, New Jersey: Princeton University Press, 1976.

Brown, Raymond. *Jesus: God and Man*. New York: Macmillan Publishing Co., 1967.

Brunner, Emil. *Man in Revolt*. Philadelphia: The Westminster Press, 1939.

Busia, Kofi. *The Challenge of Africa*. New York: Frederick A.

Praeger, 1962.

Combolin, Jose. *Retrieving the Human*. Maryknoll, New York: Orbis Books, 1990.

Cone, James, H. *A Black Theology of Liberation*. Second Edition. Maryknoll, New York: Orbis Books, 1986.

_____. *Black Theology and Black Power*. Minneapolis, Minnesota: The Seabury Press, 1969.

_____. *Black Theology and Black Power*. Second Edition. San Francisco: Harper & Row, 1989.

_____. *God of the Oppressed*, San Francisco: Harper and Row, 1975.

Davidson, Basil. *The Africans: An Entry to Cultural History*. Middlesex, England: Penguin Books Ltd., 1969.

_____. *The African Past: Chronicles from Antiquity to Modern Time*. New York: Grosset and Dunlap, 1964.

Debt Crisis Network. *From Debt to Development: Alternatives to International Debt Crisis*, Washington DC: Institute for Policy Studies, 1985.

Dickson, Kwesi. *Theology in Africa*. London and Maryknoll, New York: Dalton, Long and Todd, and Orbis Books, 1984.

_____. *Aspects of Religion and Life in Africa*. Accra: Ghana Academy of Arts and Sciences, 1977.

Diop, Cheikh Anta. *Precolonial Black Africa*. Westport, Connecticut: Lawrence Hill and Company, 1987.

Donders, Joseph, G. *Non-Bourgeois Theology: An African*

Experience of Jesus. Maryknoll, New York: Orbis Books, 1985.

Douglas, Mary, and Kaberry, Phyllis. *Man in Africa*. Garden City, New York: Anchor Books, 1969.

Downing, F. Gerald. *A Man for Us and A God for Us*. Philadelphia: Fortress Press, 1968.

Dussel, Enrique. *Ethics and Community*, Maryknoll, New York: Orbis Books, 1988.

Dwyer, John C. *Son of Man and Son of God: A New Language for Faith*. Ramsay, NJ: Paulist Press, 1983.

Ela, Jean-Marc. *African Cry*. Maryknoll, New York: Orbis Books, 1986.

_____. *My Faith as an African*. Maryknoll, New York and London: Orbis Books and Geoffrey Chapman, 1988.

Eliade, Mircea. *Myth and Reality*. New York: Torch Books/Harper & Row, 1963.

_____. *Symbolism, the Sacred and the Arts*. New York: Crossroads, 1986.

Fabella, Virginia and Torres, Sergio. *The Irruption of the Third World: Challenge to Theology*. Maryknoll, New York: Orbis Books, 1983.

Ferm, Deane William. *Profiles in Liberation Theology*. Mystic, Connecticut: Twenty-Third Publications, 1988.

_____. *Third World Liberation Theologies: A Reader*. Maryknoll, New York: Orbis Books, 1986.

_____. *Third World Liberation Theologies: An Introductory Survey*. Maryknoll, New York: Orbis Books, 1986.

Fashole-Luke, Edward, et al. *Christianity in Independent Africa*. London: Rex Collings, 1978.

Fortes, Meyer. *Religion, Morality and the Person: Essays on Tallensi Religion*. Cambridge: Cambridge University Press, 1987.

Fromm, Erich. *Marx's Concept of Man*. New York: Frederick Ungar Publishing Company, 1961 and 1966.

Fromm, Erich and Xirau, Ramon. eds. *The Nature of Man: A Reader*. New York: Collier Books, 1968.

Gallagher, Donald and Idella, eds. *The Education of Man: The Educational Philosophy of Jacques Maritain*. Notre Dame: The University of Notre Dame Press, 1962.

Gehman, Richard. *Doing African Christian Theology*. Nairobi: Evangel Publishing House, 1987.

Hadjor, Kofi B. *On Transforming Africa: Discourse with African Leaders*. Trenton, New Jersey and London: Africa World Press and Third World Communications, 1987.

Hafkin, Nancy and Bay Edna, eds. *Women in Africa: Studies in Social and Economic Change*. Stanford, California: Stanford University Press, 1976.

Hanna, Thomas. *Explorers of Humankind*. San Francisco, California: Harper & Row, 1979.

Hastings, Adrian. *Christianity in Africa*. New York: The Seabury Press, 1976.

Heilbroner, Robert. *An Inquiry into the Human Prospect*. New York: W.W. Norton and Company, 1980.

Hill, Edmund. *Being Human*. London: Geoffrey Chapman, 1984.

Hillman, Eugene. *Polygamy Reconsidered: African Plural Marriages and the Christian Churches*. Maryknoll, New York: Orbis Books, 1975.

Hopkins, Dwight. *Black Theology USA and South Africa: Politics, Culture and Liberation*. Maryknoll, New York: Orbis Books, 1989.

Iloanusi, O.A. *Myths of the Creation of Man and the Origins of Death in Africa: A Study in Igbo Traditional Culture and Other African Cultures*. Frankfurt am Main: Peter Lang, 1984.

Ilunga, Bakole wa. *Paths of Liberation: A Third World Spirituality*. Maryknoll, New York: Orbis Books, 1984.

Imasogie, Osadolor. *Guidelines for Christian Theology in Africa*. Achimota, Ghana: Africa Christian Press, 1983.

Jahn, Janheinz. *Muntu: The New African Culture*. New York: Grove Press, 1961.

Jewett, Paul K. *Man as Male and Female*. Grand Rapids: William B. Eerdmans Publishing Company, 1975.

July, Robert. *The Origins of Modern African Thought*, New York: Frederick A. Praeger, 1975.

Gordon, Milton. *Human Nature, Class, and Ethnicity*. New York: Oxford University Press, 1978.

Kato, Byang. *Theological Pitfalls in Africa*. Kisumu, Kenya: Evangel Publishing House, 1975.

Kaunda, Kenneth D. *The Riddle of Violence*, San Francisco, California: Harper & Row, 1980.

_____. *Zambia Shall Be Free*. London: Heinemann Educational Books, 1962.

_____. *A Humanist in Africa*. Nashville: Abingdon Press, 1966.

Kim, Seyoon. *The Son of Man as The Son of God*, Grand Rapids, Michigan: William B. Eerdmans Publishing Co., 1983.

Ki-Zerbo, J. *General History of Africa, Vol.1: Methodology and African Prehistory*. Abridged Edition, London and Berkeley, California (UNESCO): James Currey and University of California Press, 1981 and 1990.

Kraft, Charles. *Christianity in Culture: A Study in Dynamic Biblical Theologizing in Cross-Cultural Perspective*. Maryknoll, New York: Orbis Books, 1979.

Kretzschmar, Louise. *The Voice of Black Theology in South Africa*. Johannesburg: Raven Press, 1986.

Kuukure, Edward. The *Destiny of Man: Dagaare Beliefs in Dialogue with Christian Eschatology*. Frankfurt am Main, Germany: Peter Lang, 1985.

Lauer, Eugene, et al. *A Christian Understanding of the Human Person: Basic Readings*. Ramsay, NJ.: Paulist Press, 1982.

Lawson, E. Thomas. *Religions of Africa*. San Francisco: Harper & Row, 1985.

Liebenow, J. Gus. *African Politics: Crisis and Challenges*. Bloomington Indiana: Indiana University Press, 1986.

Luzbetak, Louis J. *The Church and Cultures: New Perspective in Missiological Anthropology*. Maryknoll, New York: Orbis Books, 1988.

Macmurray, John. *Persons in Relations*. London: Faber and Faber, 1961.

_____. *The Self as Agent*. London: Faber and Faber, 1957.

Macquarrie, John. *In Search of Humanity*. New York: Crossroads, 1985.

Mazrui, Ali A. *The Africans: A Triple Heritage*. Boston: Little, Brown and Company, 1986.

_____. *The African Condition*. Cambridge: Cambridge University Press, 1980.

McVeigh, Malcolm J. *God in Africa: Conceptions of God in African Traditional Religion and Christianity*. Cape Cod, Massachusetts: Claude Stark, 1974.

Mitchell, Robert C. *African Primal Religions*. Niles, Illinois: Argus Communications, 1977.

Mokhtar, G. *General History of Africa, Vol.ll: Ancient Civilizations of Africa*. Abridged Edition, London and Berkeley, California (UNESCO): James Currey and University of California Press, 1981 and 1990.

Moore, Basil. ed. *The Challenge of Black Theology in South African*. Atlanta: John Knox Press, 1974.

Morris, Colin and Kaunda, Kenneth. *A Humanist in Africa*.

Nashville, Tennessee: Abingdon Press, 1966.

Mosala, Itumeleng, et al. *The Unquestionable Right To be Free.*
Maryknoll, New York: Orbis Books, 1986.

Motlhabi, Mokgethi. *The Theory and Practice of Black
Resistance to Apartheid.* Johannesburg: Skotaville Publishers,
1984.

Mveng, Engelbert. *l'Afrique dans l'Église Paroles d'un Croyant.*
Paris: l'Harmattan, 1985.

Mudimbe, V.Y. *The Invention of Africa: Gnosis, Philosophy,
and the Order of Knowledge.* Bloomington, Indiana and
London: Indiana University Press and James Currey, 1988.

Murray, Jocelyn. *Cultural Atlas of Africa.* New York: Facts on
File Publications, 1981.

Muzorewa, Gwinyai H. *The Origin and Development of African
Theology.* Maryknoll, New York: Orbis Books, 1985.

Niebuhr, Reinhold. *The Nature and Destiny of Man.* New York:
Charles Scribner's Sons, 1964.

Nkrumah, Kwame. *I Speak of Freedom: A Statement of African
Ideology.* New York: Frederick A. Praeger, 1961.

Nyang, Sulayman S. *Islam, Christianity, and African Identity.*
Brattleboro, Vermont: Amana Books, 1984.

Nyerere, Julius K. Ujamaa: *Essays on Socialism.* London:
Oxford University Press, 1968.

_____. *Uhuru na Umoja: Freedom and Socialism.* London:
Oxford University Press, 1968.

Oduyoye, Mercy Amba. *Hearing and Knowing*. Maryknoll, New York: Orbis Books, 1986.

Oliver, Harold H. *Relatedness*. Macon, Georgia: Mercer University Press, 1984.

Opoku, Kofi Asare. *Speak to the Wind: Proverbs from Africa*. New York: Lonthrop, Lee and Shepard Company, 1975.

Packer, James. *Knowing Man*. Westchester, Illinois: Cornerstone Books, 1979.

_____. and Thomas Howard. *Christianity: The True Humanism*. Waco, Texas: Word Books Publishers, 1985.

Pannenberg, Wolfhart. *Anthropology in Theological Perspective*. Philadelphia: The Westminster Press, 1985.

_____. *What is Man?* Philadelphia: Fortress Press, 1970.

Parrinder, Geoffrey. *African Mythology*. London: Hamlyn, 1967.

p'Bitek, Okot. *Religion of the Central Luo*, Nairobi, Kenya: East African Literature Bureau, 1971.

_____. *Western Scholarship and the Study of African Religio*. Kampala, Uganda: East African Literature Bureau, 1971?

Pobee, John S. *Toward an African Theology*. Nashville, Tennesse: Abingdon Press, 1979.

_____, and Hallencreutz, Carl, eds. *Variations in Christian Theology in Africa*. Nairobi, Kenya: Uzima Press, 1986.

Ray, Benjamin C. African Religions: *Symbol, Ritual, and Community*. Englewood Cliffs, New Jersey: Prentice-Hall,

Inc., 1976.

Roberts, James Deotis. *A Black Political Theology*. Philadelphia: The Westminster Press, 1974.

Robinson, John. *The Human Face of God*. Philadelphia: The Westminster Press, 1973.

Ruch, E.A., and Anyanwu, K.C. *African Philosophy*. Rome: Catholic Book Agency, 1984.

Russell, Letty M. *Becoming Human*. Philadelphia: The Westminister Press, 1982.

_____. Human *Liberation in A Feminist Perspective: A Theology*. Philadelphia: The Westminister Press, 1974.

Sawyerr, Harry. *God: Ancestor or Creator?* London: Longman Group Ltd., 1970.

Schoffeleers, J.M., and Roscoe, A.A. *Land of Fire: Oral Literature from Malawi*. Limbe, Malawi: Popular Publications, 1985.

Schoonenberg, Piet. *Man and Sin*. Notre Dame, Indiana: University of Notre Dame, 1965.

Segy, Ladislas. *African Sculpture Speaks*. New York: Da Capo Press, 1975.

_____. *Masks of Black Africa*. New York: Dover Publications, Inc., 1976.

Senghor, Leopold S. *On African Socialism*. New York: Frederick A. Praeger, 1964.

Shenk, David. *Peace and Reconciliation in Africa*. Nairobi,

Kenya: Uzima Press, 1983.

Shorter, Alyward. *African Christian Theology*. London: Geoffrey Chapman, 1975.

_____. ed. *African Christian Spirituality*. London: Geoffrey Chapman, 1978.

_____. *Jesus and the Witchdoctor: An Approach to Healing and Wholenes*. London and Maryknoll, New York: Geoffrey Chapman and Orbis Books, 1985.

_____. *Prayer in the Religious Traditions of Africa*. London: Oxford University Press, 1975.

_____. *Towards a Theology of Inculturation*. Maryknoll, New York: Orbis Books, 1988.

Soyinka, Wole. *The Man Died*. London: Arrow Books Ltd., 1985.

Stevenson, Leslie. *Seven Theories of Human Nature*. Second Edition. New York: Oxford University Press, 1987.

Sundkler, Bengt. *Bantu Prophets in South Africa*. London: Oxford University Press, 1961.

Tempeles, Placide. *Bantu Philosophy*. Paris: Presence Africaine, 1959.

Temu, A. and B. Swai. *Historians and Africanist History: A Critique*. London: Zed Press, 1981.

Thomas, M.M. *Salvation and Humanization*. Madras: The Christian Literature Society, 1971.

Tienou, Tite. *The Theological Task of the Church in Africa*.

Achimota, Ghana: Africa Christian Press, 1982.

Thielicke, Helmut. *Being Human...Becoming Human*. Garden City, New York: Doubleday and Company, Inc., 1984.

Thiong'o, Ngungi wa. *Detained: A Writer's Prison Diary*. London: Heinemann Educational Books, 1981.

Tillich, Paul. *Theology of Culture*. London: Oxford University Press, 1959.

Tlhagale, Buti, and Mosala Itumeleng, eds. *Hammering Swords into Ploughshares*. Grand Rapids and Trenton: W.B. Eerdmans Publishing Company and Africa World Press, Inc., 1986.

Torres, Sergio; and Fabella Virginia. *The Emergent Gospel*. London: Geoffrey Chapman, 1978.

Twesigye, Emmanuel K. *Common Ground: Christianity, African Religion and Philosophy*. Frankfurt am Main: Peter Lang, 1987.

_____. *The Global Human Problem: Ignorance, Hate, Injustice and Violence*. Frankfurt am Main: Peter Lang, 1988.

Varga, Andrew. *On Being Human: Principles of Ethics*. Ramsay, NJ.: Paulist Press, 1978.

Viladesau, Richard. *The Reason For Our Hope: An Introduction To Christian Anthropology*. Ramsay, NJ.: Paulist Press, 1984.

Wan-Tatah, Victor. *Emancipation in African Theology: An Inquiry on the Relevance of Latin American Liberation Theology to Africa*. Frankfurt am Main: Peter Lang, 1989.

Wehrli, Eugene. *The Gospel and the Conflict of Faiths*. Boston: United Church Press, 1969.

Wilmore, Gayraud, and Cone James, eds. *Black Theology: A Documentary History, 1966-1979*. Maryknoll, New York: Orbis   Books, 1979.

Zahan, Dominique. *The Religion, Spirituality and Thought of Traditional Africa*. Chicago: University of Chicago Press, 1979.

Zuesse, Evans. *Ritual Cosmos: The Sanctification of Life in African Religion*. Athens, Ohio: Ohio University Press, 1979.

B. *ARTICLES*

Awolalu, J.O. "The African Traditional View of Man." *Orita*. Vl/2 (Dec. 1972): 101-118.

Bahm, A.J. "Ecumenical Humanism." *African Ecclesial Review*, Vol. 27, No. 2. (April 1985): 99-102.

Burleson, W.B. "John Mbiti as Anti-Historian of Theology." *African Theological Journal*. Vol.16, No. 2, (1987): 104-120.

Bimwenye-Kweshi, O. "The Advent Within the Event." *Voices from the Third World*. Vol. 2, No. 2. (1979):

Bosch, David. "Missionary theology in Africa." *Journal of Theology for Southern Africa*: No.49. (Dec. 1984):

Byaruhanga-Akiiki, A.B.T. "The Philosophy and Theology of Time in Africa: The Bantu Case." *African Ecclesial Review*:

Vol. 22. No. 6. (1980): 357-369.

Commission Theologique Internationale. "Theologie, Chris tologie, Anthropologie." *Revue Africaine de Theology*. Vol. 7, No. 13. (Avril 1983): 87-102.

Costas, Orlando. "Contextualization and Incarnation." *Journal of Theology for Southern Africa*: No. 29. (Dec. 1979): 23-30.

Edwards, Felicity. "The Doctrine of God and The Feminine Principle." *Journal of Theology for Southern Africa*: No. 37. (Dec. 1981): 23-37.

Frenkel, M. Yu. "Edward Blyden and the Concept of African Personality." *African Affairs*: Vol. 73, No. 292. (July 1974): 277-289.

Gilles, Francis. "The Bantu Concept of Time." *Religion*: Vol. 10. (Spring 1980): 16-30.

Heusch, Luc de. "Myth as Reality." *Journal of Religion in Africa*: Vol.XVIII, 3. (October) 1988.

Idowu, E.B. "Man, An Enigma." *Orita*, Vl/2, (Dec. 1972): 67-74.

Ikenga-Metuh, E. "Towards an African Theology of Man." In *African Theological Journal*. Vol.11. No. 2. (1982) 143-150.

Kapenzi, Geoffrey Z. "African Humanism in South Africa, 1850-1920..." In *Missiology: An International Review*: Vol. XVI, No. 2. (April 1988): 183-202.

Lensink, J.M. "Humanism in Africa." *Missionalia*: Vol. 2. (1974):159-167.

Lucier, Ruth M. "Dynamics of Hierarchy in African Thought." *Listening: Journal of Religion and Culture*: Vol. 24. No. 1. (winter) 1989.

Lufuluabo, R.P.F.M. "La Conception Bantoue Face au Christianisme." *Présence Africaine*. (1963): 115-131.

Maimela, S.S. "Towards a Theology of Humanization." *Journal of Theology of for Southern Africa*: No. 41. (December) 1982.

_____. "Man in 'White' Theology." *Journal of Theology for Southern Africa*: No. 36. (Sept. 1981): 27-42.

Manus, Chris U. "The Subordination of Women in the Church. 1 Cor. 4: 33b-36 Reconsidered." *Revue Africaine de Theologie*: Vol. 8. No. 16 (Oct. 1984): 183-195.

Maurrier, H. "Foi, Thelogie et Anthropologie." *Revue Africaine de Theologie*: Vol. 7. No. 13 (Avril 1983): 51-66.

Moore, R.O. "God and Man in Bantu Religion." *African Ecclesial Review:* Vol IX, No. 2. (1967): 149-160.

Ngimbi-Nseka, "Theologie et Anthropologie Transcendantale." *Revue Africaine de Theologie*: Vol. 3, No. 5. (Avril 1979): 5-27.

Nithamburi, R. "On The Possibility of a New Image for an African Woman." *Voices from the Third World*: Vol. 10. No. 1. (1987): 103-110.

Nxumalo, Jabulani. "Christ and the Ancestors in the African World." *Journal of Theology for Southern Africa*: No. 32. (Sept. 1980): 3-22.

Nyamiti, Charles. "New Theological Approach and New Vision

of the Church in Africa." *Revue Africaine de Theologie*: Vol. 2. No. 3. (Avril) 1978.

Oduyoye, M.A. "Feminism: A Pre-condition for a Christian Anthropology." In *African Theological Journal*: Vol.11, No. 3. 1982.

_____. "'In the Image of God...': A Theological Reflection from an African Perspective." In *Revue Africaine de Theologie*: Vol. 4, No. 7. 1982.

_____. "Women and the Church in Africa: Perspectives from the Present." In *Voices from the Third world*: Vol. III. No. 2. (Dec. 1980): 17-24.

_____. "Christian Feminism and the African Culture." Unpublished paper presented at Union Theological Seminary, New York, February, 1987.

_____. "Reflection from a Third Woman's Perspective: Woman's Experience and Liberation Theologies." In *Irruption of the Third World: Challenge to Theology*, edited by Torres Sergio, and Fabella, Virginia. Maryknoll, New York: Orbis Books, 1983: 246-255.

Okolo, Chukwudum. "The Church and the Nigerian Woman." *African Ecclesial Review*: vol. 27, No. 6 (December) 1985.

Olubunmi-Smith, Pamela J. "Feminism in Cross-Cultural Perspective: Women in Africa." *Transformation*: Vol. 6. No. 2.(April/June 1986): 11-17.

Omoyajowo, J.A. "The Concept of Man in Africa." *Orita*: Vol. IX/1. (June 1975): 34-48.

_____. "The Christian View of Man." In *Orita*: Vol. VI/2. (Dec. 1972): 119-129.

Omulokoli, W. "The Quest For Authentic African Christianity." In *Evangelical Review of Theology*: Vol. 12. No. 1. (January) 1988.

Parratt, John K. "Time in Traditional African Thought." In *Religion: Journal of Religion and Religions*: Vol. 7. Part Two. (Autumn 1977): 117-126.

Ray, Benjamin. "Recent Studies in African Religions." A book review article on John Mbiti, *African Religions and Philosophy*, (1970) and *Concepts of God in Africa*, (1970) in *History of Religions*: Vol. 12. No. 1. (Aug. 1972): 75-89.

Ruch, E.A. "Philosophy of African History." In *African Studies*: Vol. 32. No. 2. (1973): 113-126.

Sankey, Lugano. "African Concept of Time." In *Africa Theological Journal*: No. 2. (Feb.1969): 98-101.

Sawyerr, Harry. "Salvation Viewed from the African Situation." *Presence*: Vol. V, No. 3. (1972): 16-23.

Schoffeleers, M. J. "Black and African Theology in Southern Africa: A Controversy Re-Examined." *Journal of Religion in Africa*: Vol. XVIII. (June 1988): 29-38.

_____. "Folk Christology in Africa: The Dialectics of the Ng'anga Paradigm." In Journal of *Religion in Africa*: Vol. XIX, No. 2. (June 1989): 157-181.

Setiloane, G. M. "Confessing Christ To-day, From one African Perspective: Man and Community." In *Journal of Theology for Southern Africa*: No. 12. (September) 1975.

Shaw, Thurstan. "An Archaeological View of Man." *Orita*: VII/1. (June 1973): 3-15.

Shelton, Austine. "The Black Mystique: Reactionary Extremes
    in 'Negritude'." In *African Affairs*: Vol. 63. No. 251.
    (April 1964): 115-128.

Shutte, A. "A Philosophy of the Human Person for
    Contemporary Theology." In *Journal of Theology for
    Southern Africa*: No. 12. (September) 1975.

Sindima, H. "Community of Life" in *The Ecumenical Review*,
    41, No. 4, (1989) pp. 537-551.

Wambutda, D.N. "Savannah Theology: A Biblical
    Reconsideration of the Concept of Salvation in the African
    Context." In *Bulletin of African Theology*: Vol. 3. No. 6.
    (1981): 138-153.

Webster, John. "The humanity of God and Man: An
    Introduction to Eberhard Jungel." In *Evangelical Review of
    Theology*: Vol. 10. No. 3. (July) 1986.

Tutu, D. M. "Black Theology/African Theology: Soul Mates or
    Antagonists?" in *Journal of Religious Thought*: Vol. 32, No.
    2 (Fall-Winter 1975): 25-33.

Index